THI

Scientists and politicians have a love-hate relationship. Scientists make discoveries and give new knowledge to the world, for the benefit of humankind. But knowledge can be bought and sold. Knowledge is power, and politicians use power for their own purposes . . . which are not always for the benefit of humankind.

Malcolm Jaggard is a spycatcher, and a servant of the politicians. He's hard, and tough, and intelligent – and he wants to marry Penny Ashton, a scientist, and the daughter of the scientist George Ashton. Then the Ashtons' comfortable world is suddenly shattered, and Malcolm is ordered by his politician bosses to protect Ashton. But who is George Ashton? And how do you protect a man who has just disappeared?

Malcolm needs more knowledge, and he can't get it. So he fights for it. But knowledge is power, and servants must not have power. As his search for Ashton turns into a desperate and violent manhunt, Malcolm finds knowledge. But he also finds himself in the long-running war between scientists and politicians – a war that it is safer to keep out of, a war where
    'We have met the enemy, and he is us.'

Desmond Bagley (1923–83) wrote many fast-moving and exciting thrillers. All his novels have been bestsellers, and several have been made into very popular films.

OXFORD BOOKWORMS
Series Editor: Tricia Hedge

OXFORD BOOKWORMS

Stage 1 (400 words)

Love or Money? *Rowena Akinyemi*
One-Way Ticket *Jennifer Bassett*
 (short stories)
The President's Murderer *Jennifer Bassett*

*The Elephant Man *Tim Vicary*
White Death *Tim Vicary*
The Monkey's Paw *W.W.Jacobs*
Under the Moon *Rowena Akinyemi*

Stage 2 (700 words)

*Sherlock Holmes Short Stories
 Sir A. Conan Doyle
Voodoo Island *Michael Duckworth*
New Yorkers *O.Henry* (short stories)
The Death of Karen Silkwood
 Joyce Hannam

The Love of a King *Peter Dainty*
The Piano *Rosemary Border*
Grace Darling *Tim Vicary*
Dead Man's Island *John Escott*
Ear-rings from Frankfurt *Reg Wright*

Stage 3 (1000 words)

Go, Lovely Rose *H.E.Bates*
 (short stories)
The Picture of Dorian Gray
 Oscar Wilde
Chemical Secret *Tim Vicary*
Wyatt's Hurricane *Desmond Bagley*

Frankenstein *Mary Shelley*
*Skyjack! *Tim Vicary*
Love Story *Erich Segal*
Tooth and Claw *Saki* (short stories)
The Brontë Story *Tim Vicary*

Stage 4 (1400 words)

*The Hound of the Baskervilles
 Sir A. Conan Doyle
Three Men in a Boat *Jerome K. Jerome*
Mr Midshipman Hornblower *C.S.Forester*
Dr Jekyll and Mr Hyde *R.L.Stevenson*

Desert, Mountain, Sea *Sue Leather*
The Moonspinners *Mary Stewart*
Reflex *Dick Francis*
The Big Sleep *Raymond Chandler*
Death of an Englishman *Magdalen Nabb*

Stage 5 (1800 words)

*Ghost Stories *retold by Rosemary Border*
Heat and Dust *Ruth Prawer Jhabvala*
This Rough Magic *Mary Stewart*
Wuthering Heights *Emily Brontë*
Far from the Madding Crowd
 Thomas Hardy

The Bride Price *Buchi Emecheta*
The Dead of Jericho *Colin Dexter*
Great Expectations *Charles Dickens*
I, Robot *Isaac Asimov*
Brat Farrar *Josephine Tey*

Stage 6 (2500 words)

*Tess of the d'Urbervilles *Thomas Hardy*
Meteor *John Wyndham* (short stories)
Night Without End *Alistair MacLean*
Oliver Twist *Charles Dickens*

Cry Freedom *John Briley*
Jane Eyre *Charlotte Brontë*
The Enemy *Desmond Bagley*
Deadheads *Reginald Hill*

---

* *Cassettes available for these titles*
For a current list of titles, please refer to the Oxford English *catalogue.*

The Enemy

Desmond Bagley

retold by
Ralph Mowat

OXFORD UNIVERSITY PRESS

Oxford University Press
Walton Street, Oxford OX2 6DP

Oxford New York Toronto Madrid
Delhi Bombay Calcutta Madras Karachi
Kuala Lumpur Singapore Hong Kong Tokyo
Nairobi Dar es Salaam Cape Town
Melbourne Auckland
and associated companies in
Berlin Ibadan

OXFORD and OXFORD ENGLISH
are trade marks of Oxford University Press

ISBN 0 19 421667 5

Original edition © Literary Publications Limited 1977
First published 1977 by William Collins Sons & Co. Ltd
This simplified edition © Oxford University Press 1991

First published 1991
Third impression 1992

Illustrated by Ivan Allen/The Inkshed

Printed in England by Clays Ltd, St Ives plc

1

An interesting woman

I first met Penelope Ashton at a dinner-party. She was not a beautiful woman, but she was well-dressed, quite pretty and, as I quickly realized, very intelligent. She was a good listener, but did not say much herself. After dinner I managed to spend a lot of time talking to her. I learned that she was a biologist doing research with Professor Lumsden at University College in London. She was an attractive and interesting woman.

It was late when the party came to an end and I took her to catch the last train home.

'Which station does your train go from?' I asked.

'Victoria,' she replied.

In the taxi on the way to Victoria Station I asked her out to dinner. She was silent for a moment, then said,

'All right. Wednesday evening.'

After she had hurried off to catch her train, I realized I didn't know if she was married or not.

On the following Wednesday I met her at University College at a quarter past seven in the evening. 'Do you always work so late?' I asked.

She shook her head. 'Not always. It depends on how my work is going. Sometimes earlier, sometimes later.'

We went to the theatre and had dinner afterwards in a restaurant in Soho. For me it was a most enjoyable evening and I think it was for Penelope, too.

In the next six weeks we went out together several times

and I realized that Penelope Ashton was becoming a serious part of my life.

One evening we had dinner at my flat. I cooked a Chinese meal for her and, when she told me how much she had enjoyed the meal, she also invited me to her home for the weekend. To meet her family.

Marlow is a small town on the River Thames, about an hour's drive from London. The house where Penelope lived with her father and her sister was in the countryside, just a few minutes from the town. It was a large and beautiful house, the kind that you read about in the best magazines. It had a big, well-kept garden, tennis courts and a swimming-pool.

Penelope's father, George Ashton, was in his mid-fifties. His wife was dead and he had not married again. He was tall, grey-haired, and very fit, as I discovered when he beat me at tennis. After the game I was tired, but Ashton dived in to the swimming-pool for a swim before going back to the house for a shower. He was twenty-five years older than I was, but I was exhausted from the game of tennis, which I had lost. I sat down beside Penelope.

'Is he always like that, always so full of energy?' I asked.

'Always!' she promised.

Her sister, Gillian, was not at all like Penelope. She was the kind of woman who likes to stay at home and run the house. It was a large house, with several servants, and she organized it very well. Gillian told the servants what to do, she planned the meals, and seemed to be very happy.

It was a friendly family and I soon felt very comfortable

with them, although I knew that I was there to be inspected. We had dinner, we talked, the girls went to bed, and George Ashton and I sat and talked for a long time. He told me about his two factories, which made special kinds of plastic materials. Then he asked me, very politely, how I earned my living.

'I'm an economist,' I answered. 'I work in a company which studies economic problems and then helps other companies to do their business better. We don't work for big companies, but lots of smaller ones, like yours, find our advice useful.'

Ashton seemed happy with my answers and the rest of the weekend passed quietly. On Sunday evening, as I was leaving, Ashton invited me to return the following weekend. I was happy to accept. I had enjoyed that first family weekend, and I had enjoyed their company. Ashton, the rich, fit and independent businessman; Gillian, his home-loving daughter, and Penelope, the scientist with her own career outside the family. The only strange member of the group was Benson, Ashton's personal servant. He spoke with a gentle, educated accent but his face looked as if he had had far too many fights when he was a young man.

2

Acid in the eyes

Penelope was very busy the next week. She worked all Friday night and when I met her at the laboratory on Saturday morning, she looked very tired.

'I'm going to have to sleep this afternoon, Malcolm. It won't be much of a weekend for you, I'm afraid. But I'm sure my father will keep you busy. I'm sorry, but I'm just very, very tired.'

I was sorry, too, because I was going to ask her to marry me that weekend. However, it wasn't the right moment to put the question, so I asked her what she had been doing all night.

'Oh, we were doing a very difficult experiment, trying to transfer some dangerous genetic material.'

'Is all this useful?' I asked. 'Does it do any good, or is that a state secret?'

'Oh, no secret, but it's useful, all right. What we're doing is an important part of medical research into cancer,' she replied.

Once again I spent an enjoyable weekend with the Ashtons. We swam, we played tennis, we talked. It sounds boring, but it was, for all of us, an important way to relax from the problems of the working week.

On Sunday evening Gillian went to church and Penelope, her father and I sat talking in the garden. It was a beautiful summer evening. Suddenly we heard a scream, then another.

Ashton said sharply, 'What the devil was that?' and we all

jumped to our feet just as Gillian came round the corner of the house, holding her hands to her face. She screamed again, and fell to the grass. Ashton was the first to reach her. He tried to pull her hands from her face, but she resisted him with all her strength.

Penelope bent over Gillian, who was now lying on the grass. The screams had stopped and a faint voice murmured, 'My eyes! Oh my eyes!'

Penny put her finger to Gillian's face and then put it to her nose. She turned to her father.

'Quick, take her into the kitchen – quickly!' She turned to me.

'Ring for an ambulance. Tell them it's an acid burn.'

A faint voice murmured, 'My eyes! Oh my eyes!'

I ran to the telephone as Ashton lifted Gillian up and carried her to the kitchen. I dialled 999 and immediately a voice said, 'Emergency services.'

'Ambulance.' I gave the address and telephone number. 'It's a bad acid burn on the face,' I said.

'We'll be there as quickly as we can,' said the voice.

I went to the kitchen where Penelope was trying to clean Gillian's face. Gillian was still murmuring low cries of deep pain. I looked at Ashton. I have never seen such an expression of helpless anger on anyone's face, but there was nothing I could do there, so I went outside.

Benson was looking at the ground near the gate.

'I think someone parked his car here, sir, and waited for Miss Gillian. He must have thrown acid into her face when she walked into the garden. It looks as if he turned the car on the grass then, and drove away.'

I looked at the marks on the grass.

'I think you're right,' I said. I ran back to the house, dialled 999 again, but this time, when the voice said 'Emergency services,' I replied, 'Police, please. I want to report a criminal attack.'

The ambulance arrived very quickly and took Gillian and Penelope to hospital. Ashton followed them in his car, but before he went, I took him to one side.

'I've sent for the police. They'll come while you're at the hospital, but don't worry about that. I'll stay here until you come back.'

He seemed not to understand at first, and looked at me as if he did not even know me. I repeated what I had said, and this time he heard me.

'Thanks, Malcolm,' he replied. He looked as if he had grown ten years older in the last fifteen minutes.

Alone in the house, I poured myself a drink and sat down to think while I waited for the police. Nothing made sense. Gillian Ashton was an ordinary young woman who liked living at home, looking after her father. What possible reason could anyone have for throwing acid in her face? I thought about it for a long time and got nowhere.

After a while a police car arrived. I could not tell the two policemen much because I knew very little about Gillian and her father, and they did not seem very satisfied with what I told them. Twenty minutes later another car arrived. A policeman in plain clothes came in.

'I'm Detective Inspector Honnister,' he said. 'Are you Mr Jaggard?'

'That's right. Come in, Inspector. I've got something to show you which I'm not supposed to let you see. But in these circumstances I think I have to show it to you.'

Honnister looked puzzled as I gave him my special identity card. 'We don't see many of these, Mr Jaggard. They're rather special. Have you any ideas about what's happened? Are you here on business?'

I shook my head. 'No, I've got no ideas. I'm not here for professional reasons. I'm just a family guest for the weekend.'

'Well, this looks like the sort of problem we're going to have to solve the hard way – step by step. But I'll be glad to have your help, Mr Jaggard.'

Ashton and Penny came back some hours later. Penny

looked pale and tired, but Ashton had recovered some of his energy.

'Good of you to stay, Malcolm. Stay a little longer – I want to talk to you. Not now, but later.' He spoke as if it was an order, not a request.

He went off to his study and I turned to Penny.

'How's Gillian?'

'Not good,' she said sadly. 'It was strong acid. What sort of person could do such a terrible thing?'

'That's what the police want to know. Does your father have any enemies?' I asked.

'Daddy?' She frowned. 'If you become successful, you're bound to upset some people, so there must be some people who don't like him. But not the kind of enemy who'd throw acid into his daughter's face. That's something different.'

I had to agree, and we talked as we had our dinner – just the two of us. Shortly afterwards Benson came into the room.

'Mr Ashton would like to see you, sir,' he announced.

Ashton was sitting at his desk, a glass of whisky in his hand. The bottle in front of him was half empty.

'I'm so sorry about what has happened,' I said.

'I know, Malcolm,' he agreed. 'But, tell me, how are things with you and Penny?'

'We're very good friends. Is that what you mean?'

'Not exactly. What are your plans?' he replied.

'I intend to ask her to marry me, but I haven't done so yet.'

He rubbed the side of his face and thought for a moment. 'What about your job? Is the money good?'

'It's fairly well paid,' I replied. 'And I have a private income as well.'

'What about the future? Will you get promoted?'

'I think so. I'm trying hard.'

He was silent for a few minutes, then he went on.

'I could offer you a better job. You'd start in Australia, you and Penny, but you'd enjoy that. The only trouble is that you'd have to start almost immediately.'

He was going too fast for me.

'Just a minute,' I said, 'I don't even know if she'll marry me. I haven't asked her yet.'

'She will,' he said positively. 'I know my daughter.'

'Maybe so,' I replied. 'But I'd like to know a lot more about this job before I decide. And talk about it fully with Penny.'

Ashton was annoyed, but he tried to hide it. 'Well, we can wait a week or two, to decide about Australia. But you ought to ask her to marry you now. I can get you a special licence and you could be married by the end of the week.'

'Stop!' I said. 'You're going too fast for me. Tonight isn't the right time to ask Penny to marry me. Not after what happened to Gillian today!'

Ashton stood up and walked impatiently around the room. 'You're right, of course. It's between you and Penny, and it's wrong of me to interfere. But do ask her to marry you now, this evening.'

I stood up. 'Mr Ashton, I don't think that would be a good thing to do, especially today. I won't do it now. I'll do it when *I* think it's right.'

I left his study immediately. I did not understand why it

was suddenly so important for Penny and me to marry so quickly. There was something wrong and I had no idea what it was.

Penelope was telephoning when I entered the hall.

'I've been talking to the doctors at the hospital,' she said. 'They say Gillian's resting more comfortably now.'

'Good. I'm glad about that. Look, I'll come back tomorrow. Perhaps we can both go to visit her and see how she feels.'

3

The mysterious George Ashton

When I walked into the office on Monday morning, there was a message on my desk. My boss, Harrison, wanted to see me immediately.

'You told a policeman at the weekend who you were,' he accused me. 'Why? Your job is supposed to be secret.'

'I was at a house-party, and something horrible happened – acid was thrown in a girl's face. The police were beginning to look at me suspiciously, so I had to tell them who I was. They would have wasted a lot of time on me if I hadn't. We're supposed to co-operate with the police, aren't we?'

'Was it really necessary to tell the police about yourself?' he asked.

'In my opinion I had no choice. Damn it, I wanted to help the police.'

I walked out of his office and went back to my own, feeling very angry. Larry Godwin was there. We shared an office and were good friends. He also knew a great deal about factories and businesses in Britain.

'Do you know anything about a man called Ashton?' I asked him. 'He runs a factory in Slough. They make a special kind of plastic material.'

'I haven't heard of him,' said Larry. 'Why don't you ask Nellie? She knows everything,' he laughed.

The computer that our office used was called Nellie – I forget why. In its memory there was an enormous amount of information. I sat down in front of the screen, pushed a couple of buttons, and the words 'IDENTIFY YOURSELF' appeared on the screen.

I identified myself, and Nellie asked 'INFORMATION LEVEL?' I answered 'Green'.

All the information in the computer was kept on different 'levels'. Some people had permission to look only at information which was not very important and not very secret. That was 'Level Green'. There was other, very secret information, which could be seen only by Ogilvie, the head of the department. In between there were several different levels, each one known by a colour.

I typed in Ashton's name and address, and almost immediately the message came up on Nellie's screen.

THIS INFORMATION IS NOT AVAILABLE
AT THIS LEVEL
TRY LEVEL YELLOW

I was very surprised. I hadn't expected to find anything at

all about Ashton in the computer memory. What Nellie's message meant was that somewhere in the computer there was a lot of information about George Ashton, and that information was secret. Ashton wasn't just an ordinary businessman.

I typed my identification for Level Yellow. This was more complicated and took me four minutes. Back came Nellie's reply:

THIS INFORMATION IS NOT AVAILABLE
AT THIS LEVEL
TRY LEVEL RED

I sat back to think. I knew that information at Level Red was very secret, and I began to wonder about Ashton. Who was he? Why was everything about him so secret?

I had permission to see Level Red, but it took me ten minutes to go through the stages to identify myself. Finally I finished typing and waited for Nellie to tell me all about Penelope's mysterious father.

Instead of that, Nellie replied on the screen:

THIS INFORMATION IS NOT AVAILABLE
AT THIS LEVEL
TRY LEVEL PURPLE

Level Purple was too high, too secret for me. All I had learned about George Ashton was that something in his life or work was extremely important and secret.

A couple of hours later Larry and I were talking in our office when the phone rang. It was Harrison, our boss.

Level Purple was too high, too secret for me.

'What the hell have you been doing with the computer, you fool?' he demanded.

'Nothing much. Why? Has it broken down?' I said.

'What's all this about a man called Ashton?' he continued. 'Ogilvie wants to see both of us, immediately. Come on!'

Ogilvie was the head of our department. He was not alone. There was a short, fat man sitting in one of the chairs. Ogilvie didn't introduce him, but asked me immediately:

'Malcom, why are you so interested in George Ashton?'

'I'm going to marry his daughter,' I replied.

This statement produced a very surprising response. For a minute everybody stared at me in shocked silence. Then the fat man said:

'Why did you think information about Ashton might be in the computer?'

'No reason,' I replied. 'I didn't know anything about him and someone suggested, just as a joke, that I should look in the computer. I didn't expect to find even his name there. But something strange happened over the weekend, and I wanted to find out more about him.'

'What happened?'

'Someone threw acid into his daughter's face and . . .'

'The face of the girl you intend to marry?' interrupted the nameless man.

'No. The younger girl, Gillian. Later on, Ashton behaved strangely.'

'I'm not surprised,' said Ogilvie. He turned to Mr Nameless. 'Do you think this is serious?'

'It could be very serious, but I think we're lucky. We already have an inside man, someone in the family.' Mr Nameless pointed his cigarette at me.

'Now, wait a minute!' I said. 'I don't know what this is all about, but Ashton is going to be my father-in-law. I'm going to be a member of his family. You surely aren't going to ask me to spy on him.'

'We're not asking you,' said Mr Nameless calmly. 'We're telling you what to do.'

'Forget it! I'm not going to be a spy in my own family.'

Mr Nameless looked at me in surprise, then looked at Ogilvie and said, 'I thought you said this man was a good member of your department. I don't think I can agree.'

'I'm not worried what you think,' I replied angrily.

'Be quiet, Malcolm!' said Ogilvie. He turned to Harrison, 'You can go now, Joe.'

Joe Harrison did not look happy as he left. As the door

closed behind him, Ogilvie said, 'I think Malcolm has made an important point. An agent, someone working for the Department, should not be personally involved in a particular case. Malcolm, what do you think of Ashton?'

'I like him – what I know of him. He's not an easy man to get to know, but I've only met him on two weekends.'

'I take your point,' said Mr Nameless, suddenly more friendly. 'But we must not waste the fact that Mr Jaggard is on the inside. That could be very useful to us.'

Before I could object, Ogilvie said quickly,

'I think that Malcolm will investigate what has happened in Ashton's family as soon as he understands clearly why he should do so.'

'Yes,' replied Mr Nameless, 'but you mustn't say too much. You know the problem, and its limits.'

'I think we can keep within the limits,' replied Ogilvie coldly.

Mr Nameless stood up. 'Then that's what I'll report.'

When he had gone, Ogilvie said, 'Malcolm, you really must be careful about what you say to important officials of the government. You're too rich and independent-minded – you don't care what you say to people. Luckily, I warned his Lordship before you came in that you're not an easy person to work with.'

His Lordship! Who, I wondered, was this man? How was he so important? What did he have to do with Ashton?

Ogilvie went on, 'Take things easy now, Malcolm. Don't make any difficulties that aren't real ones. Will you do that?'

'Of course,' I replied. 'That isn't too much to ask, as long as I know what I'm supposed to do.'

Ogilvie invited me to have lunch with him so that I could tell him everything that had happened. When I had finished, he lit a cigarette and said,

'All right. You're a trained detective. Is there anything unusual about Ashton?'

I thought for a moment before replying, 'There's a servant called Benson. He seems ordinary, but Ashton doesn't seem to treat him like an ordinary servant.'

'OK,' said Ogilvie. 'Anything else that was unusual?'

'The way he asked me to marry Penelope! He was in such a hurry. He behaved almost like an old-fashioned father with a pregnant daughter.'

'You know what I think,' said Ogilvie. 'I think Ashton is frightened, very frightened. Not so much for himself, but for his daughters. One's been attacked, and he seems to think that if he can get Penny away from him, she'll be all right. That's why he suddenly invented that job in Australia for you.'

'Just a minute! I don't understand this,' I said. 'Who *is* this man, Ashton? Why are we so bloody interested in him?'

'Sorry. I can't tell you that. But I can tell you what you have to do.'

'What's that?' I asked.

'Take good care of the girl. That means also looking after the father, of course.'

'Without knowing the reason why?'

'You know why. You've got to make sure that Penelope Ashton doesn't get acid thrown in her face.'

'But I'm really guarding Ashton!'

16

'Yes, you're right there. And you mustn't let any of them know who you really are, or that you work for this department. That's going to be difficult, I know, but I can give you a team of men to help you.'

'You mean I have to guard a man and his daughter without telling them that I'm guarding them? I'll certainly need help!'

'You'll get it,' said Ogilvie, with a smile. 'Doesn't it worry you that you're marrying into such a mysterious family?'

'I'm marrying Penelope, not her father,' I replied.

4

Family problems

Later that afternoon I drove to Marlow to talk to Inspector Honnister. He looked at me curiously and a little unhappily.

'One of your people has been on the phone to tell me that I mustn't talk to anyone about you. There was no need to do that – I'm a policeman, so I know how to keep secrets.'

I cursed the stupidity of someone in Ogilvie's office who had tried to interfere, and said to Honnister, 'Look, forget all that nonsense. Last night I told you I had nothing official to do with Ashton. It was true then, but it isn't true now. My office now has a definite interest in him. I'm going to need your help.'

'I'll be happy to give it – as long as you don't try to hide things from me. What do you want to know?'

'First of all, how's the girl?'

'We're not allowed to talk to her, so she must be bad,' he replied. 'Her sister's been at the hospital most of the day.'

'Have you spoken to Ashton?' I asked.

'Yes. He says he can think of no possible reason why anyone should attack his daughter in that way. He told me nothing of any use,' replied Honnister.

'I'll see both of them later,' I said, 'and I'll try to get more information. I want to catch that man with the acid.'

'Does Ashton know who – and what – you are?' asked Honnister.

'No, he doesn't; and he mustn't find out, either,' I replied.

'That's going to give you an interesting life, with you wanting to marry his daughter, too.'

I smiled. 'Where did you find that information?'

'I'm a good policeman. One of the servants in Ashton's house was quite happy to talk about you and Miss Ashton.'

'All right. Tell me a few secrets about Ashton.'

'We've got very little. Some time ago one of our policemen talked to him about safety and how to protect his house against burglars. A waste of time. Ashton's house was already almost as well protected as the Bank of England.'

That was interesting to know. What did Ashton have that was so valuable?

Honnister went on, 'Don't forget it wasn't George Ashton who was attacked. It was Gillian Ashton. An acid attack on a woman always makes me wonder about another woman. Could it be a jealous wife getting her revenge on Gillian?'

'I've thought of that, too. Penny says it's impossible – Gillian isn't that kind of woman.'

'She may be right, but you never know. It's one of the possibilities I've got to try to find out about,' said Honnister.

'Of course. But I don't think it'll lead you to the man who threw the acid.'

'You could be right,' he replied. 'Somehow I don't think we're going to find this man easily.'

'I'm going to talk to Penelope and her father,' I said. 'Shall I meet you later on and tell you what I've learned?'

'Yes, I'd like that. I'll be in the bar of the Coach and Horses between nine and ten o'clock. See you then.'

When I arrived at Ashton's house, the gates were closed and I had to ask a guard to let me in. Neither Ashton nor Penelope was at home, but Benson told me that Penelope had telephoned to say that she would be home quite soon.

'This is a very bad business, sir, very bad.'

'How does Mr Ashton seem after the attack?' I asked him.

'He's upset, of course, sir, very upset. But he seems to be taking it very well. He went to his office this morning as usual. Can I get you a drink, sir?'

It was clear that Benson did not want me to ask him too many questions about Ashton, so I asked him to bring me a whisky. He did so, and left the room. Penelope arrived before I'd finished my drink. She looked very tired and pale.

'Oh Malcolm,' she cried. 'How good to see you.'

'How's Gillian?' I asked.

'A little better, I think. She's getting over the shock.'

'I'm very glad to hear it. I talked with Inspector Honnister, the policeman in charge of the case. He'd like to talk to Gillian as soon as possible.'

'Oh, Malcolm; she isn't ready for that yet. It's too soon.'
She came close to me and I put my arms around her.

'Are her injuries that bad?' I asked.

She put her head on my chest for a moment and said,
'You don't realize how bad this sort of thing is for a woman.
Women care much more about their appearance than men.
Gillian's got to get over two bad shocks – a psychological
shock as well as a physical one.'

'Yes, I can understand that. But Honnister needs to know
anything that Gillian can tell him. At the moment he knows
nothing, not even if the attacker was a man or a woman.'

Penelope looked surprised. 'I hadn't thought of that. And
Gillian hasn't talked about it. We've kept off the subject of
acid-throwing.'

'When you go to the hospital tonight, could you see
if she can remember anything, anything at all, about
what happened? We've got to find this person, and it's
probably better if you talk to her than if Honnister
does it. But he really does need to know what happened.
Maybe Gillian can remember something about the acid-
thrower!'

'I'll try, but I can't promise that she'll be able to tell me
anything useful.'

Penelope went to get dinner ready and I walked around in
the garden until Ashton came home. He looked worried and
tired, but there was more than that; he had the look of a
small boy who has just discovered that the world is an
unjust place – the look of a boy who has been punished for
something he hasn't done.

'Gillian's blind,' he said shortly.

'Oh no! I'm so sorry,' I replied. 'Does she know? Does Penny know?'

'Neither of them knows. And I don't want them to know until Gillian's strong enough to take the shock. So don't tell Penny.'

'I won't tell her, but she might find out for herself. Don't forget she's a doctor.'

'Well,' he said, 'I'd rather they knew later than sooner. What a terrible thing this is, Malcolm. I just can't understand it.'

'Don't you have any ideas at all?' I asked. I had to start to do my job as a policeman. I could also see that Ashton was now carrying a gun in a pocket under his arm, but I could hardly ask him about that. 'Could there be something in Gillian's life that you don't know about? Could she have become involved with some unsuitable friends?'

He became angry immediately. 'Impossible!' he said very sharply. 'Gillian's always been such a good girl. I've never had any problems with her. She's never done a thing wrong. Penny's different; she can be very difficult at times. You'll find that out if you marry her. But Gillian's never been any trouble at all.'

When Ashton said this, I understood the pain parents feel when their children are sick or when they get hurt in an accident. Then Ashton asked me if I'd thought any more about asking Penny to marry me immediately and go to Australia. I told him I hadn't changed my mind, that it was the wrong moment to present Penny with new problems.

'I suppose you're right,' he said in a disappointed voice. 'Are you staying to dinner, Malcolm?'

'With your permission,' I replied politely. 'I'm taking Penelope to the hospital afterwards.'

He nodded. 'Don't tell her about Gillian's eyes. Promise me that.'

'I already have.'

He didn't answer that, but turned on his heel and walked away towards the house. I felt very sorry for him. Whatever the information about him in the computer, I could see in his eyes the deep pain that he was suffering.

Penny and I went to the hospital and I waited for an hour while she talked to Gillian. Then we went to meet Inspector Honnister and I introduced him to Penny.

'Thank you for coming, Miss Ashton,' he said. 'We're doing the best we can in this case, but we need information and we haven't got any.'

'I understand,' she replied. 'I've got some news for you, but I don't know how much it will help you.'

'Well, Miss Ashton, let's hear what you've got,' said Honnister gently.

'Gillian says it was a man.'

'Ah!' said Honnister with satisfaction. A little more than half the population of Britain had just been dropped from his list of possible suspects.

'What sort of man? Young? Old? Anything you can tell me will be of value.'

He led Penelope through Gillian's story several times and each time managed to get a little more helpful information. Gillian had walked back from church and had seen a car parked near the entrance to the drive leading to the house. Someone was bending over the car, looking at the engine.

She thought the car had broken down and went over to offer to help. As she came up to him, the man turned and smiled at her. She had never seen him before. She was just about to speak to him when he threw the acid into her face. He didn't speak at all, but she could remember that he was about forty, with pale skin. She couldn't really say anything more about him.

After Honnister had left us, Penny and I talked a bit more about what we had learned. Then we fell silent.

'What are you thinking about?' asked Penny after a few minutes.

Automatically I said what was in my mind. 'I'm thinking it would be a good idea if we got married.'

'Malcolm!' she said, with surprise, shock, pleasure and sadness all mixed up in that one word.

'Don't you think it's a good idea?' I said and watched her try to find words to reply. 'But don't say, "This is so sudden!"'

'But that's exactly what it is, so sudden,' she said, 'and here, of all places!'

'Does the place matter?'

'I don't suppose it does,' she said quietly. 'But the time does. Why now?'

'I suppose I could have picked a better time,' I agreed. 'But the question just jumped out of my mouth. You asked me what I was thinking about. Actually, I'm not the only one who thinks it's a good idea. Your father does, too; he wanted me to ask you last night.'

'So you two have been discussing me behind my back. I don't know that I like that.'

'Don't get angry. It's traditional – and polite – for a man to talk about his plans with his probable future father-in-law.'

'What would you have done if he had been against it?' asked Penelope.

'I'd have asked you just the same. I'm marrying you, not your father.'

'You're not marrying anyone – yet.' She laid her hand on mine. 'You idiot – I was beginning to think you'd never ask.'

'I was going to, but other things got in the way.'

'I know,' she said sadly. 'I've been so unhappy today, thinking about Gillian and seeing her in so much pain. And Daddy – he doesn't say much, but I think he's going through hell. And now you come and give me more problems.'

'I'm sorry, Penny. Perhaps I should take the question back. Forget about it for now.'

'No,' she said. 'You can't unask a question.' She was silent for a while, and at last she said, 'I will marry you, Malcolm – I'd marry you tomorrow, but that can't be. I don't know when it will be. We've got to get this business with Gillian sorted out first. Can you wait?'

'Of course,' I replied happily.

As we drove to her home, my heart was like a singing bird and I realized the truth in all that the poets say about love.

'I think we should tell your father. He seems to be worried about you,' I suggested, just before Penny went in.

'I'll tell him now,' she said as she gave me a goodnight kiss.

5

Ashton disappears

Ogilvie wanted me to protect Ashton and his family, so early next morning I was in the office making my plans. I went to Ogilvie and told him that the first thing I needed was a list of all the people Ashton was in contact with.

Ogilvie smiled and pushed some papers across the desk. 'It's all there, ready for you.'

In return I gave him my list. 'That's what I need,' I said.

He looked carefully at what I had written.

'What's this? Six men, six cars, radio telephones . . .' He stopped. 'Who do you think we are – the CIA? Why do you need all these?'

'I have to watch three, perhaps four, people, twenty-four hours a day.'

He stopped me. 'Which three or four people?'

'First Ashton and Penny Ashton. Then Gillian Ashton. And Benson.'

'Why Benson?' Ogilvie demanded.

'Well, the computer has them all, even Benson, kept under 'Top Secret'. I put all the names through the computer until I lost them in Level Purple.'

'OK. But you can't keep an eye on four people with six men. I'll let you have eight. And I'll arrange for Ashton's telephones to be tapped.'

He looked at the list again. 'But what the devil do you need a gun for? Is it really essential?'

'Well, Benson's carrying a gun in his pocket, and Ashton's

got another under his arm. If they're expecting that kind of action, then we should be prepared.'

'Right, I give you permission to take two guns. Get your men together and I want a tape-recording of what you say to them.'

I called together all the men I wanted for my team and told them what they had to do. Larry, who shared my office, was one of them. It was going to be his first job in the field, away from the office.

I took the tape-recording back to Ogilvie.

'I've got another question,' he said. 'Did you cancel a request made to Inspector Honnister for copies of his reports on the Ashton case?'

'Yes. It seemed to me a waste of time, especially if I'm going to be there watching Ashton. Honnister wasn't very happy about it, and I think it's important to keep him happy. We want him to co-operate with us.'

'You're perfectly right, of course,' said Ogilvie. 'Except for one thing. This department did not request those copies. The request came from another department, and they're not very pleased that their request has been cancelled.'

'Oh,' I said. 'Who wanted the reports?'

'Do you need to ask?' said Ogilvie sharply. 'The gentleman you met yesterday is making sure he knows everything that happens. All right, Malcolm, go and look after Ashton. But don't do anything without talking to me about it first. Is that agreed?'

'Yes, I'll do that, sir.' And I left his office.

Driving back to Marlow I explained to Larry Godwin more about what had happened. I told him that information about Ashton was locked up in Level Purple in the computer, and that I didn't have permission to see it. Larry was both angry and amazed.

'It's so stupid,' he interrupted. 'You mean Ogilvie won't tell you what this business is all about?'

'I don't think he's allowed to tell me anything. There was a top man from the Government in his office when he spoke to me – obviously a man with a lot of power.'

'You mean Cregar?' he said.

I glanced quickly at him. 'Who?'

'Lord Cregar. Short fat man. I saw him coming out of Ogilvie's office when you were there yesterday. He got divorced last week – his picture was in the newspaper.'

'Do you know anything more about him?' I asked.

'Not a thing.' And he left me even more puzzled than before.

When we arrived at the hospital, we met Inspector Honnister in the car park. He looked a bit more cheerful than the day before.

'We're making progress. I think we know the make of the car. A witness saw a dark blue Ford Cortina parked near Ashton's house on Saturday afternoon. I'm beginning to think we might find this man. I hope Gillian Ashton will be able to identify him, when we get him.'

'She won't,' I replied, shaking my head. 'She's blind.'

Honnister looked horrified and swore violently.

'Wait till I catch this man. It'll be a real pleasure to send him to prison for a long, long time.'

While we were talking, Jack Brent, one of the other members of my team, came across. 'Penny Ashton's inside the hospital, visiting Gillian,' he said. 'But there's something else you ought to know,' he went on. 'We can't find Ashton.'

'Isn't he at his office?' I asked sharply.

'No, and he isn't at home. There's no sign of Benson, either.'

'Come on, Larry, quick. We're going to Ashton's house. There may be nothing to worry about, but let's make sure. Jack, stay close to Penny Ashton. For God's sake, don't lose her.'

At Ashton's house we found only one of the servants, Mary. She told us that Ashton's bed had not been slept in the previous night, and she hadn't seen him at all that day. I began to get worried and rang the hospital to speak to Penny.

'Did you tell your father about us last night?'

'No. He'd gone to bed when I got in. And he'd gone out when I got up this morning. Why? What's the matter, Malcolm? Has something happened to him?'

'I don't know if anything's happened, but I think you'd better come home now.'

'I'm coming at once,' she replied, and put the phone down.

I walked into Ashton's study. On his desk were two envelopes; one addressed to Penny and the other to me. I picked up mine and opened it.

My dear Malcolm,
You are too intelligent not to have understood what I have tried to say to you in our recent conversations.

28

There is an old French saying: 'The man who finds a good son-in-law gains a son, but the man who finds a bad one loses a daughter.' Marry Penny and make her happy – but, for her sake, be a bad son-in-law.

Yours

George Ashton

I sat down with a heavy feeling in my stomach and the knowledge that we had made a bad job of looking after Ashton.

6

A bad son-in-law?

I rang Ogilvie and told him that Ashton and Benson had disappeared, and I read him Ashton's letter.

'A bad son-in-law?' said Ogilvie. 'What the hell does he mean?'

'I think he's saying that he's getting away from Penny in order to protect her,' I said. 'I wouldn't do what he wanted – marry her at once and take her away from him – so he's taken himself away from her. He must think she's in danger if she's with him.'

'I suppose you could be right, but it seems a bloody strange way to protect his daughter. Does she know?' asked Ogilvie.

'Not yet. She's on her way back from the hospital now. Ashton's left a note for her, too. If there's anything important in it, I'll let you know.'

'Think she'll tell you?' he asked.

'Yes. The funny thing is, sir, that last night I did ask her to marry me, and she accepted. She was going to tell Ashton when she got home, but he'd already gone to bed. Maybe he'd already left. If he'd only waited another couple of hours, he might have decided not to go.'

'Well, don't blame yourself for that.' There was a pause. 'Does Penelope know about your work for the Department?'

'No,' I replied.

'Well, she has to know, and now's the time to tell her. What I want you to do is to search the house very carefully. See if you can find anything that might show where Ashton has gone. If there's anything you don't understand, bring it back to the office. I think there's going to be a lot of trouble over this.'

I didn't look forward to explaining to Penny about my work and why we wanted to search her father's house. I had a feeling that our relationship was about to change for the worse.

Just then I heard Penny's Aston-Martin sports car coming up the drive to the house. I met her as she ran to the door. Jack Brent's car was now coming up the drive.

'There's a man following me!' Penny cried, and then she noticed Larry Godwin in the hall.

'What's happening? Malcolm, who are these men? What's happened to Daddy?'

'As far as I know he's all right,' I said and took her into

her father's study. I picked up the letter. 'You'd better read this.'

As she read the note, her face turned pale. 'But I don't . . . I don't understand.'

'What does he say?' She gave me the letter and went over to the window while I read.

My dearest Penny,
For reasons which I cannot explain I must go away
for a while. I am not a criminal, and I have done
nothing wrong. I do not know how long I shall be
away, but please do not try to find me and do not
bring the police into this. My reasons are private.
I shall be quite safe because my old friend, Benson,
will be looking after me. It would make me very
happy if you would marry Malcolm as soon as
possible. I know that you love him and I think he is a
very good man. I am sure that the two of you will
be very happy together, and I am equally sure that
you will both look after Gillian. Please forgive me for my
sudden departure, but it is in the best interests of all
of us.
Your loving father
George

I looked up. 'I'm sorry, Penny.'

'But I don't understand,' she cried. 'Oh, Malcolm, what's happened to him?'

She came into my arms and I held her close. 'I don't know,' I said, 'but we'll find out.'

She was still for a while, but pushed me away as two cars arrived quickly. 'Malcolm, who are all these men? Have you told the police? Daddy said not to.'

'No, I haven't told the police,' I said quietly. 'Sit down, Penny. I have a lot to tell you.' I hesitated, not knowing best where to begin.

'I told you I work for a company called McCulloch and Ross, and that's perfectly true. We do the work I told you about – and we do it very well. But the company is also a sort of secret government department which deals with economic and industrial information if it is important to the state.'

'You mean you're some kind of spy.'

'No, not a spy.'

'But you were watching my father like a common spy,' she said angrily. 'And was I just a means to an end? Did you get close to me just to learn more about my father?'

'No!' I looked her straight in the eyes. 'I didn't know anything at all about your father until yesterday. And I don't know much more now.'

She looked at me coldly. 'And these men in the hall – are they from your department too?'

'Yes.'

'Then I'd like to talk to the man in charge. I knew something was worrying Daddy. Now I know where it was coming from.'

'You're talking to the man in charge, and you're wrong about your father,' I said carefully.

That stopped her, and she sat down suddenly. '*You* are in charge?'

'That's right.'

'And you don't know what you're doing?' she said with a laugh of disbelief.

'I know what I'm doing, but I don't know why. It's become very complicated. Let me tell you how I got into this.'

So I told her everything. I told her about Nellie the computer and the secret colour levels. I told her about Ogilvie and Cregar. I told her much more than I should have told her. I told her how, after the acid attack on Gillian, I was told to watch and protect her father.

'I've not done a very good job so far,' I said. 'But I'll find him.'

'You're not going after him? He said in his letter . . .'

I interrupted her. 'All I know is that your father is considered by some people to be a very important man. I don't know why. But he could be going into danger without realizing it. My job is still to find him and protect him. He's not in a position to do that properly himself.'

She started to cry, quietly at first, and the tears ran down her face. Then she began to tremble, as if she was suddenly very cold, and I put my arm around her. She held on to me tightly. When your safe, comfortable world seems to be falling apart, you need to hold on to somebody.

'Oh, Malcolm, what am I to do?'

'You must do what you think best. If you trust me, you'll help me to find him, but I couldn't blame you if you refuse. I haven't been open and honest with you – I should have told you all this yesterday.'

'But you couldn't – you weren't allowed to. Malcolm, what are your men waiting for?'

'For your decision. I want to search the house, and I can't do that without your permission.'

She came back to the desk and read her father's letter again.

'He wrote to me, too,' I said, and gave her my letter.

She read it slowly, then gave it back to me.

'Bring in your men,' she said, in a voice which had no expression or feeling in it.

We found a number of surprising things in that house, but none of them seemed to be of any use to us. There was no clue to tell us where Ashton could have gone. In the cellar there was a very well-equipped laboratory, but none of us had any idea what sort of work Ashton had done there. Hidden behind a cupboard in Ashton's bedroom, was a heavy steel door with the sort of lock you usually see only in banks. By measuring the walls, outside and inside the house, we discovered that there was a small, secret strong-room there – so secret that not even Penny knew about it.

While the other men were searching the house, Penny and I talked about her father's life. I asked her how long Benson had worked for the family.

'He's been with us since before I was born,' she replied. 'He used to work in one of Daddy's factories, but he visited us at least once a week. Then when we came to live in this big house, he came to live here and work as Daddy's personal servant.'

We were still talking when Peter Michaelis, one of my searchers, came in to report that they had found nothing useful, but that in a room upstairs there was the biggest model railway he had ever seen. I didn't believe him, and forgot all about it, because Ogilvie rang to tell me to come back to the office as quickly as possible. I explained about the secret strong-room and the laboratory, and he promised to send some experts immediately to examine everything.

Before I left I looked for Michaelis and found him with the model railway.

'You haven't time to play with that,' I said angrily. 'We're here on business – to find out about Ashton.'

Michaelis smiled. 'This *is* business. To search this place thoroughly we'll have to look inside every piece of this railway set. The whole thing is so big that we have to use the controls to bring everything back to this central point.'

I looked at the railway more carefully. It was very big, and very complicated – all controlled from a central desk. There must have been about two kilometres of railway line, but Michaelis seemed to know how to work the controls, so I left him to search the thousand different pieces of equipment, and went downstairs.

Penny was waiting for me, her eyes flashing with anger. 'Someone has been searching my room.'

'I know,' I replied. 'All the rooms in the house have been searched.'

'I think you could have trusted me,' she said icily.

'It's not a question of trust,' I tried to explain. 'I do my job in the way I was taught. I have to go by the book.'

'Then it's not the kind of book I'd want to read,' she exploded, and we had our first big quarrel.

The model railway was very big, and very complicated.

7

Ashton and the Russian scientist

I was not in the best of tempers when I met Ogilvie back in the office an hour later. All I could tell him was that Ashton had obviously been prepared for escape for a long time. He had been frightened of something and had made his plans carefully, ready to be put into operation at any moment.

Ogilvie had another problem. 'I had a meeting this afternoon with the Minister and people from other departments. It wasn't easy; there are other people who don't want our department to be in charge of Ashton's case.'

'Lord Cregar, for example?' I asked.

'How did you recognize him?'

'He gets his photograph in the papers,' I replied.

'Well, his interest in Ashton goes back a long time. Before this department started, Ashton was dealt with by Cregar's department. Cregar badly wants to take Ashton's case away from us. However, today the Minister decided that Ashton was still our case, and so it's still our job to find him. That means it's *your* job, Malcolm.'

'I need permission to see Level Purple in the computer.'

'Not possible!'

'Don't be stupid,' I replied angrily. 'How can I look for a man if I don't know anything about him. Either I get to see Level Purple tomorrow or I resign.'

'You're always in too much of a hurry, Malcolm. To begin with, I couldn't get permission for you to see Level Purple by tomorrow, and in any case, Ashton isn't in Level

Purple. He's in Level Black. And you couldn't get permission to see Level Black in less than three months.'

'That's it, then,' I said. 'I'd better go along to my office and type my resignation.'

'Don't be a young fool!' Ogilvie said sharply. He thought for a long minute, drumming his fingers on the desk. Suddenly he said, 'I've made up my mind. But if anyone ever knows of this, I could lose my job. Wait here.'

He went through a door at the back of his office, was away for several minutes and then returned.

'Come in here.'

I followed him into a small room where there was a computer screen.

'I've opened Level Black for you,' he said. 'You must read about Ashton, and only Ashton. There are other things in Level Black which are better for you not to know.'

'You have my word.'

He nodded and left, closing the door behind him.

I looked at the computer screen. On it was a message: *No written notes to be made of anything in Level Black.*

I sighed and started to read about George Ashton's life, which had been a very full one.

Aleksandr Chelyuskin was born near Novgorod in Russia in 1919. At the age of twelve he was such a good student that he was sent to a special school in Moscow where he made excellent progress, especially in mathematics. In 1936 he came under the influence of Peter Kapitza, a brilliant Russian physicist, who had studied for some years in England. Kapitza changed the direction of Chelyuskin's studies from

mathematics to physics, and Chelyuskin later played an
important part in improving the quality of Russian weapons
in the war of 1939–45.

In March 1945, when the Russians discovered that the
Americans had developed the atomic bomb, Chelyuskin was
told to work on the development of a similar bomb for
Russia.

After the war finished in 1945, Chelyuskin became
dissatisfied because he had to go on working on research
into weapons, and he did not like what he was doing. He
began to think about people, not physics and mathematics.
He decided that he did not like Russian society and the
direction which Russia was following after the war.

He decided to kill himself, but without actually dying. He
made a careful and complicated plan, and three months later
it was reported that he had died in a fire. The burnt body of a
man was certainly found after the fire, but it was not
Chelyuskin's.

So, at the age of twenty-eight, Chelyuskin arrived secretly
in England. Unfortunately for the English, who had hoped to
learn about Russian secrets from him, Chelyuskin refused to
talk about his work on atomic weapons. He did not want to
work as a scientist for the British Government. What he
wanted to do was to live in England as an ordinary citizen.
The government officials and scientists who had been
looking forward to his ideas could not understand him, but
finally he got what he had asked for. He did almost exactly
the same as he had done in Russia; he took another man's
identity – this time an English soldier who had died in a
traffic accident. Chelyuskin was taught to speak English, and

when he finally took the place of the George Ashton who had died, he was able to live successfully as a member of English society.

It was a strange new world for 'George Ashton'. At first he took a job in a shop, but this quickly bored him. He had been given some money to help him in his new life, and soon he started a business with a man whom he met at work. John Franklin was good at working with his hands, 'George Ashton' was good at using his brains, and their business did well. Ashton married Franklin's daughter, Mary, and they had two daughters, Penelope and Gillian. Two years later Mary Franklin died and Ashton looked after the two girls. At the same time he worked hard to develop new chemical materials for industry, which gradually made him very rich.

All this time people from the British Secret Service were watching carefully to see if the man from Russia would do something extraordinary with his brilliant scientific mind. But Ashton concentrated on his business, and gradually the officials from the government lost interest in what he was doing. Ashton became more and more successful in industry, but no one paid much attention, until I had sounded the alarm by my careless questions to the computer. Until then the life of George Ashton, previously Aleksandr Chelyuskin, my future father-in-law, had run very smoothly in England.

When I finished, I had been sitting in front of the computer screen for two and a half hours and I had a headache. I went back to Ogilvie's office where he offered me a glass of whisky and we sat down to talk about what I had seen.

'What do you think?' he began.

'I think George Ashton is one hell of a man. I'm proud to have known him,' I replied.

'Anything else?'

'Yes,' I said. 'One fact. There's been a big change in the kind of scientific work Ashton has done in England. It's all technical; he's been applying his own earlier ideas to developing new materials. But that isn't the type of person he was before. He was a man who thought up new ideas – everything he did, all of his training was in that direction. Did he just give it up when he came to England? Or has he been applying his mind to something that we don't know anything about?'

'You're not too stupid,' said Ogilvie. 'You're probably right. You can't stop a man thinking, but how can you find out what he's been thinking about?'

'Do we know what books he buys, what scientific magazines he reads?' I asked.

'Yes, he keeps up to date only in the type of chemistry that is important to his business. Nothing else.'

We sat for a few minutes in silence and then I asked, 'What does Cregar have to do with Ashton?'

'It was his department that helped Ashton escape from Russia after the war. Cregar himself went into Russia to bring him out. Cregar wasn't Lord Cregar then; his name was Pallton. Now he's head of his department. When Ashton became an ordinary businessman instead of a scientist with lots of valuable secrets, his records were

41

moved to our department and Cregar was very annoyed. He always thought that Ashton might do something scientifically useful one day. Although Cregar brought Ashton out of Russia, Ashton never really liked him, and certainly didn't trust him. That's probably why Cregar's interfering now. He's sure that Ashton has useful ideas that he's hiding from everybody.'

'Is there any news of Ashton?' I asked.

'None at all. We've got people watching the airports and the ports – all the usual things,' replied Ogilvie. 'We must find him.'

'And I want to find the man who threw the acid into Gillian Ashton's face, and frightened Ashton so much that he ran away to protect his children from any more attacks.'

The next day brought little progress. Penny wouldn't speak to me after our quarrel about the search of her room and nobody had seen Ashton or Benson at any of the airports or seaports.

At three o'clock Ogilvie rang me to say that they expected to unlock the strong-room at Ashton's house later that afternoon.

'I want you to be there. Listen carefully! When the door is finally opened, only you and the man working on the lock will be present. As soon as the door is opened, you send him out of the room and check what is inside the strong-room. If the contents can be moved, you bring them here. If they can't be moved, you close and lock the door again. No one else must see what is in that room. Is that clear?'

'Perfectly clear,' I replied.

When I arrived at the Ashtons' house once again, I met

Lord Cregar in the hall. He did not look pleased to see me.

'Ah, Mr Jaggard. I understand there is a strong-room here. Has it been opened yet?'

I wondered where he got his information, but answered, 'No, not yet.'

'Good. Then I am in time,' said Lord Cregar.

I said, 'Am I to understand that you wish to be present when the room is opened?'

'That's correct,' he replied.

'I'm afraid that will not be possible.'

He looked at me thoughtfully. 'Do you know who I am?'

'Yes, my lord. I have instructions that nobody except myself is to be present when the door is opened.'

His eyes opened wide with surprise and anger.

'Did Ogilvie say that?'

'Those were his instructions to me. I don't know if he was thinking of you, my lord. Do you wish to speak to him? There is a telephone in the study.'

'Yes,' he replied. 'I'd better speak to Ogilvie myself.'

He went off to the study and I went over to the window and looked out at the garden. A few minutes later Cregar came out of the study, looking very angry. He left the house, got into his car and drove quickly away.

The phone rang. It was Ogilvie. 'Cregar must not be allowed into that strong-room and he mustn't know what is inside.'

'He won't,' I replied. 'He's gone. We're just about to open the door.'

'Let me know what you find,' he said.

I went up to Ashton's bedroom.

'There you are,' said the man who was working on the door. 'You can open it now.'

'I'll have to ask you to leave now, Frank,' I told him.

He went out and closed the bedroom door behind him.

I opened the door to the strong-room.

Ogilvie's mouth fell open.

'Empty?'

'Absolutely!' I replied. 'There wasn't a thing in that room. It looks as though it's never been used since it was first built.'

'Who else knows about this?' he asked.

'No one. Only you and I.'

'That's a pity. Cregar will never believe me when I tell him. Perhaps I should have let him stay with you.'

I didn't care what Cregar believed or did not believe, but Ogilvie warned me to be careful.

'Cregar is a bad man to have as an enemy. He didn't like the way you treated him today.'

'He didn't show it. He seemed pleasant enough,' I replied.

'That's his way,' said Ogilvie. 'Always polite and pleasant. But don't trust him.'

8

The man who threw the acid

After that nothing happened for a while. The search for Ashton and Benson continued, but with no success. The day after we opened the strong-room, I rang Penny.

'Is this to tell me you've found Daddy?' she asked.

'No. I've got no news about him. I'm sorry.'

'Then I don't think we've much to talk about, Malcolm,' she said, and rang off.

Gillian was still in hospital and I went to visit her. The doctor said there was a chance that she might recover some of the sight of her left eye, but she would never see with her right eye again. When I talked with Gillian, she wanted to know what had gone wrong between Penny and me.

'Nothing,' I said lightly. 'Did she say there was anything wrong?'

'No, but she stopped talking about you, and when I asked, she said she hadn't seen you.'

'We've both been very busy,' I said.

I changed the subject and we talked about other things. Afterwards I spoke to Peter Michaelis, who was the member of my team with the job of protecting her. He found the job boring, but told me he tried to help Gillian by reading to her every afternoon. He was a kind man and he and Gillian had become quite friendly. When we talked about Ashton, Michaelis said that the most interesting thing he had seen in the house had been the model railway – by far the largest he had ever seen.

'He's got copies of all the old railway timetables and the system runs to time. It's very complicated, so he's got a computer, and he's managed to program the whole timetable on it. It's wonderful. The whole thing works automatically.'

That sounded like Ashton – find the most efficient way to do something. However, his railway system was not helping me to find him, so I left Michaelis and went back to London.

Two weeks after Ashton had disappeared, Honnister rang me.

'We've got a suspect. A man in London. He hired a car for the weekend when Miss Ashton was attacked. The owner of the car-hire firm told one of our men that acid had been spilt on the back seat.'

'What's the man's name? Has he said anything yet?' I demanded.

'His name's Mayberry. One of the men from Scotland Yard is going to see him this evening. He's an Inspector Crammond.'

'I'll ring him at once. I want to be there to make sure they aren't too bloody soft with him.'

I met Crammond that evening and we went to Finsbury in North London where Mayberry lived in a small flat.

'He doesn't sound like a violent man,' said Crammond. 'The woman who owns the house describes him as very quiet, always reading. And he goes to church twice on Sundays.'

I felt disappointed. This sounded less and less like our man. We went up to the flat and knocked on the door.

A man in his forties, with a pale, unhealthy skin, opened the door.

'Mr Peter Mayberry?' said Crammond.

'Yes,' came the reply.

'We're police officers,' said Crammond pleasantly. 'We think you can help us. Can we come in?'

'I suppose so. How can I help you?' he asked coldly.

It wasn't a very luxurious flat. The furniture was either old or cheap but it was clean and tidy. On one wall there was a shelf with forty or fifty books on it. I looked at them. Some were about religion, some were about the protection of the world from scientific progress, others were ordinary stories.

Crammond started by asking to see Mayberry's driving licence.

'I don't have a car,' replied Mayberry.

'That wasn't what I asked,' said Crammond. 'Can I see your licence, please?'

Mayberry took his licence out of his jacket pocket and handed it over. Crammond examined it carefully and passed it to me.

'When did you last drive a car, Mr Mayberry?' asked Crammond.

Mayberry said, 'Look, if anyone says I've been in an accident, they're wrong, because I haven't.'

He seemed nervous.

'Do you ever hire a car?' continued Crammond.

'I have done.'

'Recently?'

'No. Not for some months,' replied Mayberry.

'Supposing I said that you hired a car in Slough two weekends ago, what would you say?' asked Crammond.

'I'd say you were wrong,' replied Mayberry quietly.

'Where were you that weekend?'

'Here – as usual. You can ask Mrs Jackson downstairs.'

Crammond looked at him for a moment. 'Mrs Jackson was away that weekend. Did anyone see you? Did you go to church?'

'No, I didn't feel well.'

Crammond spoke more strongly.

'Mr Mayberry, I suggest that you are telling me lies. I think that on Saturday morning you went to Slough by train and you hired a Ford Cortina car from Joliffe's garage. Mr Joliffe was very angry about the acid damage to the back seat of the car. Where did you buy the acid?'

'I bought no acid,' said Mayberry.

'But you hired the car. You gave your name and address to Mr Joliffe.'

'No,' repeated Mayberry.

'Well,' said Inspector Crammond, 'we can easily check that. We have the fingerprints from the car. I'm sure you won't mind coming to the police station so that we can compare yours with those from the car.'

This was the first I had heard of fingerprints and I was not sure that Crammond really had any, but it worried Mayberry.

'I don't have to give you my fingerprints. I want you to leave, or I'll . . .'

'Send for the police?' said Crammond. 'When did you first meet Miss Ashton?' he went on suddenly.

'I've never met her,' said Mayberry quickly. Too quickly.

'But you know of her,' insisted Crammond.

Mayberry was very nervous now. He took a step backwards and bumped into the table, knocking a book onto the floor. I picked it up and looked at the front. *A Report on Developments in Genetics.* Suddenly a number of puzzling facts began to make sense to me. Mayberry's basic religious ideas, his interest in protecting the world from modern science, and what I knew about the work Penny Ashton was doing.

I said, 'Mr Mayberry, what do you think of what is happening in modern biological science?' Crammond looked very surprised.

Mayberry turned to look at me. 'It's bad,' he said. 'Very bad.'

'In what way?' I asked.

'The biologists are breaking the laws of God,' cried Mayberry. 'They are creating new forms of life, life that is not in the Bible, life that was not made by God.'

Mayberry was becoming more and more excited now.

'She's godless. She's destroying the work of God and making monsters.'

I had difficulty in keeping my voice calm.

'I suppose that by 'she' you mean Dr Penelope Ashton?'

Crammond looked very puzzled by now; the change of direction in the conversation had left him behind. Mayberry, now in a state of extreme nervous excitement, said thoughtlessly,

'Among others.'

'Such as Professor Lumsden?' I replied.

'He's her boss, her devil!'

'If you thought she was doing wrong, why didn't you talk to her about it? Perhaps you could have made her change her mind, see things your way,' I asked.

'She would never have listened to me, and I wouldn't want to talk to her,' said Mayberry.

Crammond realized what was happening.

'Mr Mayberry,' he said, 'are you admitting that you threw acid into the face of a woman called Ashton?'

Mayberry had a hunted look on his face now as he realized that he had said too much.

'I haven't said that.'

'You've said enough.' Crammond turned to me. 'I think we have enough information now to take him to the police station.'

I nodded, then said to Mayberry,

'You're a religious man. You go to church every Sunday – twice, I'm told. Do you think it was a good action to throw acid into the face of a young woman?'

'I am not responsible to you for my actions,' said Mayberry. 'I am responsible only to God.'

'And may God help you,' I said. 'Because you got the wrong girl. You threw the acid in the face of Dr Ashton's sister, who was coming home from church.'

Mayberry stared at me. The confident expression on his face now changed to an expression of absolute horror.

He whispered, 'The wrong . . . wrong . . .'

Suddenly a kind of horror overcame him, his whole body shook and he screamed at the top of his voice before falling heavily to the floor, unconscious.

'Oh damn!' said Crammond as the policeman waiting outside burst into the room. 'He'll never go to prison now.'

Mayberry was now lying on the floor, crying and making noises which neither Crammond nor I could understand.

'He's mad. Phone for an ambulance,' said Crammond. 'We'll not get any more sensible answers out of him.'

9

Lord Cregar again

Next morning I told Ogilvie about Mayberry. He found it difficult to believe and asked lots of questions.

'Did he throw the acid just because he thought she was doing something wrong? Are you sure? Could someone else have told him to do it? Why did he choose Dr Ashton?' Ogilvie's questions came like bullets from a gun.

'We can't be absolutely sure,' I replied. 'The man's completely mad now and I don't think we'll ever learn much more from him.'

'Damn it, Malcolm. The whole thing doesn't make sense. If this bloody fool chose a scientist by chance, and then threw the acid in the face of the wrong girl, why did Ashton run away?'

I had no answer to that. We seemed to have made no progress at all in the search for George Ashton.

I went along to the university to tell Penny. She was with Lumsden, her boss, but took me to her own office. Her manner to me was cool.

'What do you want here, Malcolm?' she said. 'Have you found Daddy?'

I shook my head. 'We've found the man who threw the acid,' I said.

'Oh!' She sat down at her desk. 'Who is he?'

'A man called Peter Mayberry. He works in an office in London. He's also a very religious man.'

She frowned, then said, 'But whatever could he have to do with Gillian?'

I sat down. 'I'm sorry, Penny. I didn't want to tell you this, but you have to know. The acid wasn't intended for Gillian. It was intended for you.'

'For me!' She shook her head as if she couldn't believe what I had said. 'Why on earth should a man like that want to attack me? Why me?'

'He seemed to think that you were interfering with the laws of God.'

Suddenly she realized the full meaning of what I had said.

'Oh, my God!' she cried. 'Poor Gillian.'

Her body began to shake and her head fell forward across her desk. She began to cry loudly. I got her a glass of water, but there wasn't much I could do until she had got over the first shock. I put my arm round her and said, 'Here, drink this.'

She raised her head and cried, 'Oh, Gillian. She'd be . . . all right . . . if I . . . if I hadn't . . . Oh Malcolm; what am I to do?'

'Do? There's nothing you can do. You carry on as usual,' I said firmly.

'I don't see how I can do that? Not after this!'

I spoke carefully. 'You can't blame yourself for what happened. You mustn't think that you're responsible for the actions of someone who's crazy.'

'Oh, I wish it had been me,' she cried.

'No, you mustn't ever say or think that. Now, you've got to think clearly because I need your help. I need to ask you and your boss some questions.'

She nodded sadly and went to wash her face while I called Professor Lumsden. When he came in, he looked at Penny's white face and red eyes.

'What's happened here? And who are you?' he asked in a shocked voice.

'I'm Malcolm Jaggard and I'm a sort of police officer. I'm also engaged to Penny. We're going to be married.'

Lumsden looked very surprised. 'Oh, I didn't know about that.'

'You can't blame yourself for what happened,' I said.

53

'You know, of course, about the recent attack on Penny's sister.'

'Yes, a most terrible thing.'

I told him about Mayberry and a worried look came over his face.

'This is bad,' he said. 'I'm deeply sorry, Penny.'

'Can you tell me something about your work here, Professor?' I said.

'In a way this crazy man is right,' he said. 'We've discovered ways of isolating some of the thousands of genes in the seeds of plants and animals. Then we try to transfer them. It can be very dangerous, but if it works, it will help to produce more and better food in the world. But we are very, very careful. It's terribly important that these new bacteria can't escape from the laboratory until we are absolutely sure they're safe. Some people think we're doing wrong, because it's dangerous. Others, like your Mayberry, have religious reasons for wanting to stop us.'

I could see that Professor Lumsden had nothing to tell me that would help me find George Ashton. Penny was still very shocked and upset, so I drove her home.

Weeks and then months went by. The police and my department looked very carefully into Mayberry's life and decided that he really was mad. It had been his own idea to throw the acid and no one else had sent him. His attack had absolutely no connection with George Ashton, which left us with a big problem. Why had Ashton run away? It didn't make sense.

My relationship with Penny improved, although neither of

us referred to marriage. Gillian's condition improved a little and the doctors managed to save about a quarter of her eyesight. She was able to leave hospital and live at home. She and Penny began to make plans to go to the United States where the doctors would try to repair the damage to her face.

One evening, when Penny and I were having dinner, she said,

'Do you remember you once talked about someone called Lord Cregar?'

'Yes, that's right. Why?'

'He's been seeing my boss, Professor Lumsden.'

That caught my interest. 'Was it anything to do with Mayberry?' I asked.

'No,' replied Penny. 'The first time he came was just after you opened the strong-room in our house.'

Something seemed wrong to me. Why had Cregar been seeing Lumsden before we knew about Mayberry? Was there a connection between Ashton and Lumsden that we had missed?

10

Tragedy in Sweden

Ogilvie sent for me next morning and showed me a photograph of a man wearing a heavy coat and a fur hat. There was a lot of snow in the picture. 'Have you seen that man before?' he asked.

'Yes. That's George Ashton,' I replied.

'No, it isn't,' he said. 'That man's name is Fyodr Koslov, and he lives in Stockholm. At least, that's what his passport says.'

He passed another photograph across the desk. I took one look at it and said, 'That's Benson.'

'Are you quite sure? These photographs came from our man in Sweden. We didn't have any good recent photos of Ashton and Benson, so you're the only person who can really identify them.'

'I'm quite sure. Those are photographs of Ashton and Benson. What do you want me to do now?' I replied.

'I want you to go to Stockholm. First of all, talk to our man there, a man called Henty.'

'And then? Do I contact Ashton? Tell him about Mayberry? Tell him it's safe to come back to England?'

'No, it might frighten him if he knows that we are still watching him, even after thirty years. Just watch him and find out what the hell he's doing in Stockholm.'

Ogilvie didn't know it, but he had just made the worst mistake of his career.

It was dark and cold in Stockholm at that time of year and it never stopped snowing. I felt very cold and wondered why Ashton had decided to come to such a place.

Henty, the man who had taken the photographs of Ashton and Benson, was our only man in Stockholm and it was impossible for him to keep an eye on both of them for twenty-four hours a day. I had to go to the British Embassy to ask for assistance.

The man I saw was called Cutler. He did not like me.

'Mr Jaggard,' he said, 'we haven't got men free to do casual police work. Why is this man Ashton so important? I've never heard of him.'

'I'm not allowed to tell you anything more about him. He's too important.'

He didn't like that and refused to give me any more men to watch Ashton. So I telephoned Ogilvie in London and told him about the difficulties that Cutler was making for me. An hour later Cutler suddenly appeared at my hotel and arranged for several men to help me.

We watched Ashton and Benson very carefully – and they did nothing unusual. Ashton visited museums, went to the theatre and to the cinema, and he spent a lot of time in bookshops. The only strange thing about them was that they did nothing strange. It was as if they were on holiday. I began to wonder if Ashton was having his first ever holiday from the problems of his business life in England.

Four weeks went by like this – a boring time for all of us, and Cutler began to complain that his men were wasting their time. One day, however, Henty came to see me with news that worried me. He had discovered that we were not the only people who were watching Ashton. There was a team of other watchers who also followed Ashton everywhere he went. The next morning Henty and I followed one of them when his duty period was finished. We were horrified to find that the man went back to the Russian Embassy.

I rang Ogilvie to tell him what we had discovered. He, too, was horrified and caught the next plane to Sweden. We sat down to talk about this new situation.

'Look,' he said, 'maybe we're making too much out of all this. For thirty years Ashton has run his business quietly in England. He hasn't given us any of the wonderful scientific ideas we hoped for. If he wants to leave England, maybe even go back to Russia, why should we stop him? Why not let him do what he wants?'

'Why not?' I agreed. 'I can't say I understand what's been happening, and I'm beginning to feel that we shouldn't really be involved in this.'

'On the other hand,' continued Ogilvie, 'there are two things that puzzle me, and worry me. Why did he run away? And why did he build that strong-room, and then not use it? Why was it empty, Malcolm? Why had it never been used?'

'I've spent a lot of time asking myself the same questions. I still don't know the answers,' I replied.

'That's what worries me. Ashton is a very clever man. He's very good at making people look, and think, in the wrong direction. That's how he was able to leave Russia in the first place. Maybe he's pointing us in the wrong direction. He's trying to make us believe that he has no secrets. That could mean that there *is* something hidden, something that could be very important.'

'Then why the hell did he build the strong-room in the first place?' I said, confused.

'To deceive us. So that whoever found the strong-room would think they were wasting their time. He wanted us to think that because the secret room was empty, there was no secret information to hide.'

'But you think there may be something secret – some

scientific discovery – hidden in another place?'

'Maybe. Even probably. But I don't know for sure,' said Ogilvie. 'In any case I can't take the risk of leaving George Ashton for the Russians. I don't know why they're following him, but if they ever find out that he's really Chelyuskin, they'll be very interested, and they'll want him back. Like us, they'll want to know what scientific ideas he's been having in the last thirty years. I can't afford that risk. So we've got to take Ashton back to England whether he likes it or not.'

'I could go and tell him the Russians are following him,' I suggested. 'He'd come with us willingly then.'

'I don't know,' replied Ogilvie. 'If he thought the British Secret Service was still following him after thirty years, he might get so angry that he'd go back to Russia willingly. No, that's not good enough. It's too risky.'

'But if he finds out that the Russians are watching him, he'll probably go straight back to England,' I said.

'Provided that he doesn't know about *us*,' growled Ogilvie suspiciously. 'How do you plan to arrange it? Ask the Russians to wear flags in their hats?'

'Wait a minute!' I said. 'I've got an idea.' I turned to Larry Godwin, who had come to Stockholm with Ogilvie. 'How well do you speak Russian, Larry?'

'That depends on what kind of regional accent you want,' he replied. 'Why?'

Ogilvie began to understand. 'I see,' he said thoughtfully. 'The Russians are very careful when they watch Ashton, too careful to make mistakes. But we could make a mistake for them, and frighten Ashton away from them. I like the idea.'

59

We considered our plan carefully and three days later we put it into operation.

The situation outside Ashton's flat was becoming crazy. Two men from the British Embassy were looking in shop windows waiting for Ashton or Benson to come out. . . They did not know that they were being watched by two Russian agents looking in other shop windows. And the two Russians were being watched by two men from our department. There was hardly any room left for tourists in that narrow street.

At half-past ten that morning Ashton came out and walked towards the centre of the city. Larry Godwin, and everybody else, followed him. Ashton went into a bookshop and as he was looking at a book, Larry, who had gone in behind him, dropped a book and swore loudly in Russian. Ashton put his book back on the shelf and left the shop immediately. He walked around the streets for quite a long time, looking behind him frequently, and then went to have lunch in a restaurant. Larry followed him into the restaurant and sat down at a table near Ashton. When Larry ordered his meal, he spoke Swedish with a strong Russian accent. Ashton looked very worried and finished his meal rather quickly. Larry came out of the restaurant close behind Ashton and followed him back to Ashton's flat, making sure that Ashton could see that he was being followed.

After Ashton had returned to his flat, we had a long wait in the cold. We all had little radio-telephones and at ten to nine in the evening I received the message we had been waiting for.

'Ashton and Benson have left the flat. They're carrying bags and walking towards the taxis at the end of the street.'

Benson took a taxi to the railway station but Ashton went off in the opposite direction. At the station Benson bought two tickets for Göteborg, in the west of Sweden. There was half an hour before the train left, but Ashton did not appear and when the train went only Benson was on it, together with several of my men. Ashton had disappeared again.

I decided to follow the train by car. If Benson had bought two tickets, maybe Ashton intended to join him at the next station. I sent two men to the first station where Benson's train would stop, and Larry and I drove to the next station, Eskilstuna. On the way we heard on the radio-phone that Ashton had, in fact, got on the train at the first stop. I relaxed again.

'We've got them now,' I told Larry.

But when we arrived at the railway station at Eskilstuna, we learnt that Ashton and Benson had jumped from the train when it stopped near a small country village. I looked at the map. The nearest town was called Strangnäs and we arrived there about an hour later. It was a small town, with only one hotel. Henty knew it quite well because it was also an army training centre which he had visited officially. He went into the hotel and found that Ashton and Benson were definitely there, probably fast asleep in their rooms.

We booked into the hotel, too, and I made my plans for the next morning. I wanted Michaelis, Brent and Henty to be early for breakfast; I would be sitting in a car outside the hotel. Brent would have a secret radio-microphone and would talk quietly into it so that he could tell me what was happening. Half-way through breakfast Larry was to go in and make Ashton think that the Russians had succeeded in following him, even to Strangnäs.

The next morning I waited in the car. I hated what I was doing. I wanted to go and talk to Ashton, to tell him everything that had happened, and convince him that he had run away from England for the wrong reasons. I wanted to explain to him that the acid attack on Gillian had been a mistake made by a madman, and that it had nothing at all to do with him. I wanted to persuade him that it was completely safe to go back to England and take up his normal family and business life again.

But Ogilvie did not want that. He did not want Ashton to know that he was still being watched by the British Secret Service. And I had to do what Ogilvie said, even if I disagreed with him. At the same time, I liked George Ashton, he was Penny's father, and I hated myself for what I had to do.

Michaelis, Brent and Henty went to have breakfast in the hotel at half-past seven. A quarter of an hour later Ashton and Benson came into the restaurant and sat down for breakfast. Five minutes later Larry Godwin arrived and spoke to the waitress in Swedish with a very strong Russian accent. Ashton noticed him and went very, very pale. As Larry followed the waitress to the table, he greeted Ashton in a friendly manner, but in Russian, and Ashton knocked over his cup. I listened to Brent's description of what was happening, and I felt sick at what we were doing to George Ashton.

Ashton and Benson left the restaurant and a few minutes later they were outside the hotel. Larry followed them and did not try to hide. Ashton did not seem to know what to do and, on the radio, I told Larry to ask Ashton to go with him. At first it seemed that Ashton was going to do this, but Benson shook his head and tried to get Ashton away. Finally they started to walk out of town, towards the forest. Over the radio came Larry's voice: 'I talked to Ashton and he was ready to come with me, but Benson spoiled it. He didn't want to listen to what I had to say.'

'What are they doing now?' I asked.

'They've just left the road and walked into the forest.'

We all followed them into the trees. They kept changing direction to try to get away from us and twice we nearly lost them. After we had gone about three kilometres into the forest, I heard the sharp sound of guns. From where I was standing I could not see Ashton, but Henty was further ahead. Over the radio he said,

'It's the Swedish Army. This is a training area, and Ashton is walking straight towards the guns. He'll get himself killed.'

I started running as fast as I could. I had to stop George Ashton and I did not care what Ogilvie said. I ran on until I thought my chest would burst. I shouted.

'Ashton – George Ashton – stop!'

He stopped and turned round and his eyes grew wide with surprise. I had almost reached him when there was a single shot and Ashton fell. I heard Henty run past me as I bent over Ashton. There was blood coming from the corner of his mouth.

'Malcolm . . . what . . . ?'

'Take it easy, George,' I said, holding him up in my arms.

He pulled his hand from his pocket with a piece of paper. 'The . . . the . . .' Then he fell back, his eyes still open, looking at the sky. George Ashton was dead.

I knelt there in the snow thinking how badly I had done my job. I cursed Ogilvie and wished I had done what my own mind had told me was right. But it was too late. I had never felt so bad in all my life.

Henty came back with a gun in his hand. 'I got him,' he said.

'Got who, for God's sake?'

'Benson.'

I stared at him. '*You shot Benson?*'

He looked at me in surprise. 'Well, he shot Ashton, didn't he? I saw him do it. Maybe you couldn't see him, but I did.'

This was almost too much for me. '*Benson* shot Ashton!'

'Yes. He tried to shoot me, too,' said Henty. 'And if anyone shoots at me, I shoot back.'

I was still trying to take this in when there was a loud noise at the top of the hill above us and a huge army vehicle appeared. It stopped in front of us and a Swedish officer climbed out. Henty threw his gun on the ground as I looked at the piece of paper that Ashton had tried to give me. It was a railway timetable for trains from Stockholm to Göteborg.

The Swedish police were not happy. They had two dead bodies and four live men in the middle of an army training area. They took us to an army centre where we were kept for the next three weeks. I had no idea what was happening back in London, but suddenly, early one morning, I was told to get dressed and was taken to Stockholm Airport. The officer who had come with me said, 'There is your plane, Mr Jaggard. You are no longer welcome in Sweden.'

I arrived at Heathrow Airport in London and was met by Ogilvie. He took me to my flat and told me to report to his office the next morning. As I got out of the car, I asked him about Penny. He told me that she was away in Scotland.

'Does she know?' I asked.

'Yes,' Ogilvie said quietly. He put a piece of paper in my hand and said, 'You ought to read this.' Then he drove away.

The piece of paper contained a short article from a newspaper, which described how two Englishmen, George Ashton (56) and Howard Benson (64), had died in an unfortunate accident in Sweden. They had walked into an army training area by mistake and been killed in the gunfire.

11

More mysteries and new dangers

In Ogilvie's office the next morning I had to go over everything that had happened – from my arrival in Stockholm until Ashton's death. Ogilvie wanted to be sure of every detail. The mystery was Benson. Why had he shot Ashton? He had worked for Ashton for more than twenty years. What possible reason could there be for killing him so suddenly? Ogilvie had studied every known fact of Benson's life, and had found nothing wrong, nothing strange, nothing even slightly suspicious.

Ogilvie told me I had to attend a meeting with people from other departments the next day. He reminded me that officially I did not know of Ashton's background as Chelyuskin, because that was in Level Black of the computer, which I was not supposed to have read.

The meeting on the next day was difficult. All the people there seemed to be the heads of other departments which had been embarrassed by what had happened in Sweden. The most difficult questions came from Lord Cregar.

'Is it correct that Mr Ogilvie told you not to let Ashton know who you were?'

'Yes, that's correct,' I replied.

'But we have just been told that you showed yourself to him deliberately. It was only when he saw you that he turned back. Is that not so?'

'That's correct.'

'So it was when you disobeyed Mr Ogilvie's orders that Ashton was killed?'

I was very angry, but kept my voice calm. 'Ashton was going straight into the army training area, which was very dangerous. The most important thing was to stop him. It was a complete shock to me that Benson killed him.'

'But we can't be sure that Benson killed Ashton,' objected Lord Cregar.

'The bullets from the body prove that,' said Ogilvie.

'But Mr Jaggard has failed throughout this operation. He let Ashton escape in England, and he has now caused a great deal of trouble because of the stupid way he tried to deal with Ashton in Sweden. I said once before that I did not have a very high opinion of Mr Jaggard, and I think I was right.'

'I said once before that I did not have a very high opinion of Mr Jaggard, and I think I was right,' said Lord Cregar.

I felt very miserable and wondered if Cregar was right.

After the committee meeting Ogilvie invited me to lunch, not because he was sorry for me and not because he wanted to be friendly. To my great surprise he wanted to continue to investigate the Ashton case, and that was to be my new job. As far as everyone else was concerned, I had made a terrible mistake and I had to be punished. But Ogilvie thought that his department had been tricked over Ashton. He wanted to know who had tricked him and why. And he thought that I was the best man to find this out. I was not at all happy with this plan. It would mean more lying to Penny, and I had done enough damage to our personal lives already. Ashton had been killed and I felt that I was responsible for that. Ogilvie disagreed.

'You didn't kill Ashton. Who did?'

'Benson killed him, damn it!'

Ogilvie raised his voice to a shout. 'Then find out why, for God's sake! Don't do it for me, do it for Penny. Find out why Benson, who lived so long in the same house with her father, with her and her sister – find out why Benson killed her father. You owe that to her!'

'All right,' I said. 'You've convinced me. I'll do it for her!'

After I left Ogilvie, I said goodbye to the people I had worked with in the department. They felt sorry for me, because my new job was, as far as they knew, as a messenger, but there were no messages for me to take. In fact, I went off to start the investigation which Ogilvie wanted me to do. I went out to Marlow to find out if Penny was back from Scotland. As I arrived, I bumped into Peter Michaelis, who was just leaving the Ashton house.

'What the devil are you doing here?' I asked.

'Playing model trains,' he replied happily. 'Miss Ashton gave me permission to use the set upstairs whenever I like. It really is a fantastic railway. Here, look at this book.' He showed me a thick book of railway timetables. 'Ashton was trying to run this old timetable, but it doesn't seem quite correct. It's not the same as the original timetable, so I'm going to try to compare his timetable with one that I've got at home.'

'Which Miss Ashton gave you permission to do this?' I asked.

'Gillian,' he replied. 'I used to talk to her a lot when she was in hospital. When she found I was interested in the model railway, she said I could come along and play with it. She's a nice girl and we get on very well.' He paused. 'I don't spend all my time with the railway.'

I smiled. 'Is Gillian here now?'

'Yes, she is, and she's expecting Penny home for lunch.'

Penny was very pleased to see me. Ogilvie had told her that I had been on some secret job in the United States when her father was killed. I was very grateful for this lie. It made it easier for me to avoid telling her too many direct lies. Penny asked me if I knew anything more about her father's death. I told her that I knew little more than she did.

'But why had he gone to Sweden, Malcolm? You were investigating him. Didn't you find out anything at all?'

'Not really. At first we thought that he had run away because of the attack on Gillian. But when we found that man, Mayberry, that idea led nowhere. As far as we know, your father was having a long, quiet holiday in Sweden. There was nothing wrong in that, but we still don't know why he ran away so suddenly. We'll probably never know.'

'I suppose you're right, Malcolm. But what he did was so strange; it wasn't like him at all. I'm still very puzzled, and worried. I need time to think about it – and to think about us, too.'

'I can understand that,' I said, 'and I don't mind. It's been a terrible time for you and Gillian. What is she going to do?'

'We're both going to America soon, and the doctors there

will try to repair the damage to her face. The house is going to be sold while we're away.' She fell silent, and, afraid that she would ask more questions about her father, I changed the subject again.

'What were you doing in Scotland?' I asked.

'Oh, I was asked to advise on the building of a new laboratory. I think it needs to be P4, and they only want to go to P3.'

'I don't understand,' I said. 'What are P3 and P4?'

'Oh, I forgot. I'm so used to talking about my work with Daddy, I'd forgotten you don't know much about genetics. Daddy always seemed to understand what I was talking about so easily. Are you sure you want me to explain?' She looked at me doubtfully. 'It's a bit technical.'

'Yes, please,' I replied. 'I'm not a complete idiot, but don't make it too complicated.'

'Well, in 1975 scientists studying genetics were very worried by the possible dangers of the experiments that were being done. There were no government laws to follow, but everyone felt that something had to be done. So the scientists agreed among themselves about safety and the kind of experiments that should be permitted. For the first time scientists became their own "police", and did not wait for governments to make laws for them.

'Genetics laboratories go from P1 to P4. P1 is the ordinary, basic genetics laboratory; P4 is for highly dangerous experiments where everything has to be totally safe in all possible conditions – airlocks, showers, changes of clothing, that sort of thing.'

'And your problem in Scotland is all about safety?'

'Well, they've got a P2 laboratory and the work they do is changing. I believe they need to make it a P4 laboratory, but that's very, very expensive, and they only want to go to P3.'

'Why is that?' I said.

'Well, they want to work with bacteria called *E. coli*, which are harmless; everyone has millions of them in his body. It's not dangerous to study them. But nobody knows what could happen if someone does an important experiment and transfers the wrong gene. Everything is so new in this branch of science. There are no laws, at least no man-made laws, to decide what should be done and what should not be done.'

'But you're the expert. If you think it's dangerous, surely people will listen to you,' I said, puzzled.

'Not necessarily. In the end it's the politicians who tell you how much money you can spend, how safe you can make an important laboratory. But their reasons are not usually scientific.'

Everything always seems to come back to money and politicians, I thought to myself. Are they really the best people to decide?

12

The secret computer

Somewhere the key to Ashton's death lay in Benson's life, and I decided to investigate everything about Howard Benson. Ogilvie had told me that there was no information in the computer about Benson, but I remembered putting all the Ashton names – and Benson's – through the computer right at the beginning. Benson's records had been there then, but locked away in Level Purple. What had happened to them? Had somebody taken Benson's records out of the computer? It was a puzzle I couldn't solve, so I went to the War Office to see if I could look at Benson's army records from thirty years before. All I knew was that Benson had been a soldier during the war, but I had no idea when he had left the army. It took several hours of searching through long lists of names and numbers before I discovered, to my total amazement, that Ashton and Benson had left the British army on exactly the same day, 4th January 1947. I knew from the computer that 'George Ashton' was not a real British soldier, but a Russian scientist in disguise. The coincidence was too great. So, if it wasn't a coincidence, it must have been planned. But who had planned it? Was Benson another Russian? What reason could there be to explain why he had left the army on the same day as George Ashton, and then worked for and lived with Ashton for more than thirty years?

I took Benson's army file home and read it very carefully. Everything seemed normal, exactly as Ogilvie had found when he had investigated Benson. Then I suddenly noticed one strange point. When Benson's departure from the army was first mentioned, an officer had written, 'Proposed leaving date – 21st March 1947', but Benson had actually left on 4th January, 1947. Was the difference important?

The health of every soldier is carefully watched and recorded and I looked at Benson's medical record in the army. Early in November 1946 he had complained that he had pains in his left arm. In December the doctor had asked for a special examination of Benson's heart. And three weeks later, in January 1947, Benson had left the army!

I telephoned a friend of mine who was a doctor. 'If a man in his early thirties complains of a pain in his left arm for three months, what could be wrong with him?' I asked.

'That depends,' he replied. 'It could be one of several things. If it's a friend of yours, tell him to go to a doctor at once.'

'Why? Is it so serious?'

'It could be a kind of heart disease,' he replied.

'Is that bad?' I asked. 'Would the man survive?'

'That depends again,' said the doctor. 'Is he fit? Does he smoke?'

I remembered that Benson had had a desk job in the army. 'Let's suppose that he's not fit, and that he smokes.'

'Then he could drop dead at any time, if he doesn't get the right treatment immediately. Malcolm, is this someone I know?'

'No,' I replied. 'There was a man in that condition in 1946. He died a few weeks ago, thirty years later. What do you think of that?'

'I'm very surprised. Most people with that condition would have died long ago.'

The next person I spoke to was Benson's last doctor in Marlow. He was not keen to tell me about Benson's health, but I asked him when Benson had last had a heart attack.

He laughed and said, 'I can certainly tell you about that. There was absolutely nothing wrong with Benson's heart; it was in excellent condition.'

I thanked him and rang off. It was now fairly clear to me what had happened. The real Benson had suffered from a bad heart and had died after 18th December 1946, and before 4th January 1947. Somehow a new healthy Benson had taken his place, had left the army on 4th January, and had then remained very close to George Ashton until the day, thirty years later, when he had killed him. I had learned something, but I still did not know why Benson had killed George Ashton.

It was time for Penny and Gillian to leave for America. They had decided to sell the house at Marlow and the auction was going to be held while they were away. Gillian expected to be in America for quite a long time, but Penny hoped to be back after a week or two. She was then supposed to go back to visit the laboratory in Scotland.

It was about this time that I began to feel that somebody had given me quite a lot of valuable information, but I had failed to recognize its full importance. What was it? I thought about it for hours, but the right piece of information refused to come to the surface of my mind. Something I had heard, or maybe something I had read, was the key to the problem, but I could not find out what it was, no matter how much I tried.

On the day of the auction I went to the Ashtons' house near Marlow. To my surprise Michaelis was there, looking as unhappy as I felt.

'I'm glad Gillian isn't here to see this,' he remarked, as we looked around the rooms full of articles for sale. 'It's all so sad to see everything being sold off like this, but the model railway interests me. I thought I'd like to buy a bit of it, but I don't think I'll have a chance. Lucas Hartman is here.'

'Who's he?' I asked.

'A rich American who collects model railways. He'll buy the whole thing, I expect. It'll probably cost him £15,000, maybe more, but he'll buy it.'

'So much? Over £15,000 for a model railway? I don't believe it,' I said.

'Wait and see,' replied Michaelis. 'And what annoys me is that I never got to understand the system. Ashton's timetables didn't fit. You remember I showed you his big books of railway timetables – the old London, Midland and Scottish Railway?'

'Yes, I remember. You were going to compare them with the original ones. Weren't they the same?'

'No, they're completely different. The pattern of Ashton's timetables doesn't seem to be like any normal system of railway timetabling. I just couldn't understand it.'

As Michaelis was talking, I had a picture in my mind of George Ashton as he lay dying in the snow, trying to give me a Swedish railway timetable. It was as if a bomb exploded in my head.

'By God, that's it,' I whispered. 'That's got to be it!'

Michaelis stared at me. 'What's wrong?'

'Come on,' I said. 'We've got to speak to the auctioneer.'

Five minutes later we were talking to the man in charge of the auction.

'I'm speaking for the Ashton sisters, Penelope and Gillian. You mustn't sell the model railway upstairs.'

'I'm not so sure I can do that,' said the auctioneer. 'You say you speak for the Ashton sisters. Can you prove it?'

'No, I can't, at the moment.'

'I'm sorry, Mr Jaggard,' he said, 'I was engaged by Miss Penelope Ashton to sell the contents of this house. I can't stop that without a letter from her.'

'But she's in the United States,' I almost shouted.

'Then there's nothing to be done,' he said. 'The sale must go ahead.'

I tried ringing Ogilvie, Penny's lawyer, even Penny herself in America, but I could find none of them. Finally I rang my bank manager.

'What can I do for you, Mr Jaggard?' he asked.

'Later this afternoon I'm going to write a fairly large cheque – more than I have in my bank account at the moment. I want to borrow enough money to cover a cheque for £20,000, or even £25,000, for a month. Can I do that?'

'Yes, I don't see any difficulty, Mr Jaggard. We'll cover your cheque. I hope you know what you're doing. In any case, come and see me tomorrow about it. I'll need your signature on some papers.'

I put the phone down. Michaelis was looking at me as if he thought I had suddenly gone mad.

'Listen,' I said. 'I think we've found Ashton's secret hiding place. I think that model railway is a computer – a sort of mechanical computer. You couldn't understand Ashton's railway timetables; you said they didn't fit the original ones. Well, I don't think they're timetables at all. They're computer programs, and that's where Ashton had been hiding all his original thinking. That's what he was trying to tell me when he gave me that Swedish railway timetable just before he died.'

Michaelis shook his head. 'It's a crazy idea,' he said slowly, 'but I suppose you might be right.'

'I hope to God I *am* right,' I said. 'I'm taking a big risk – a very expensive risk!'

We went back to the room where everything was being sold. The auctioneer was just starting to sell the railway.

'Ladies and Gentlemen, this is a unique model railway, with the most modern control equipment. It is one of the finest examples of model railways that we have ever seen. How much will you offer me for it?'

The offers started at £8,000 and went up slowly to £15,000. Hartman had said nothing, but suddenly he offered £16,000. I held up a finger, and the auctioneer said, 'I have seventeen thousand pounds. Will anyone offer me more than seventeen thousand pounds?'

Hartman raised his finger to offer £18,000.

The only two people crazy enough to spend so much money for a model railway were Hartman and myself. The price went up and up. Finally I won, Hartman stopped, and the auctioneer called out,

'Sold to Mr Jaggard for £31,000!'

Just as I was talking to the auctioneer, Michaelis called me to the telephone. It was Ogilvie.

I told him what I had done. I told him that the department now owed me £31,000 for a model railway. I do not wish to write down the words that he used to describe me.

13

Ashton's work and Benson's secret

From America Penny wrote to say that the operations on Gillian's face were going well. She said that Gillian wanted me to pass this news on to Peter Michaelis, as she could not write herself.

In her next letter Penny asked me to meet her at Heathrow Airport and that made me feel a lot better. If she had decided not to marry me, she would not have asked me to meet her.

When I met her she was very tired, but I took her to her new flat in London and we sat talking for a while. She told me about her visits to several American universities.

'They're doing very good work with PV40,' she said.

'What's PV40?' I asked. 'Something to do with genetics?'

'Oh, it's a virus – but it's harmless to human beings,' she laughed. 'I keep forgetting that you don't know anything about genetics.'

Suddenly the little worrying thought at the back of my mind expressed itself.

'When your father was alive, did you talk to him a lot about your work?' I asked.

'Oh yes,' Penny replied. 'All the time. He knew quite a lot about it and he understood things very quickly. He even made some suggestions which surprised Professor Lumsden.'

'Why was that?'

'Well, Daddy never did any experiments in genetics. He learned things from talking with me. But some of the ideas he had were very clever. They were unusual, but they worked when Lumsden and I tried them out in the laboratory.'

I felt like a man who has just found a key after looking for it for many weeks.

The next day I went to see Ogilvie.

He had been very suspicious of my ideas about the model railway, but he had agreed to investigate it. The railway had been moved to a secret place and the computer experts had begun work on it. At first they thought it was a great joke, of course, but after a while they realized that it was definitely a computer and that the timetables were detailed programs. Unfortunately, they had not been able to understand the programs yet, but at least I was not £31,000 the poorer.

I told Ogilvie about my latest idea.

'I think we can guess what Ashton's computer programs are all about. The date of the first one is about the time Penny started her research in genetics. I believe Ashton taught himself genetics because that was what his daughter was studying. He used her books and her notes, and didn't need to buy anything which would tell outsiders what he was studying. She could keep him up to date with the latest developments without anyone ever suspecting that he was busy learning the subject – probably even better than Penny herself knew it. And all without ever going near a laboratory.'

'If you're right,' said Ogilvie, 'what do we do about it?'

'Talk to Penny, of course,' I said. 'Tell her what we think; see if she agrees. Let her tell us what she knows.'

'No, that's too risky,' he said. 'We'd have to tell her too much about her father and why he wanted to hide what he was doing.'

'But you can't keep this secret from her, not if you want to understand it. She's a part of it now. He learned everything from her,' I said angrily.

'Calm down, Malcolm. I didn't say anything about secrets. I just said we'd have to be very careful about what we say. You can leave that side of things to me, so don't worry about it.'

After that meeting I had a strange suspicion that Ogilvie was not being completely honest with me. It was the first time I had ever felt that about him, and I didn't like it.

I went to see Penny that afternoon at University College. As I passed Professor Lumsden's office, Lord Cregar came out. He looked very surprised and demanded, 'What are you doing here?'

I didn't think it had anything to do with him, and replied, 'Just visiting.'

He stopped and said, 'You know the Ashton case is closed?'

'Yes, of course,' I replied.

'Then you know you shouldn't be coming here to ask questions.'

'I'm sorry, Lord Cregar, but I don't think I have to ask your permission when I want to visit the girl I'm going to marry.'

'Oh!' he said. 'I'd forgotten.' His eyes changed and lost their suspicion. 'I'm sorry about that. I'd forgotten that you're engaged to Dr Ashton. I wish you both every happiness. But now, I must go, I'm in a bit of a hurry.'

As he hurried off along the corridor, I wondered why his first thought on seeing me was to think it had something to do with the Ashton case.

That evening Penny invited me to dinner in her new flat. After dinner, as we were sitting having coffee, she said quietly,

'When would you like us to get married, Malcolm?'

That night the coffee got spilt on the carpet, and I stayed for breakfast.

The next day Penny had to go to Scotland because she was still involved in arguments about the safety of the laboratory there. For me the rest of the week went by very slowly. I bought some tickets for the theatre for the day when Penny was due to return, and I went on with my work. I had learned nothing new about Benson, and the computer experts were not making much progress towards understanding Ashton's programs. Ogilvie seemed to be avoiding me, but I did learn from him that Lord Cregar was now trying to persuade the Minister to transfer the work on the computer programs from Ogilvie's department to Cregar's.

That worried me a lot. Cregar's special interest was in biological and chemical weapons. If Ashton's programs were really about genetics, as I thought they were, they could be very useful to Cregar – and he would make sure they were kept very secret. Perhaps that was why Ashton had hidden them so well – to keep them from dangerous people like Cregar who would use them only to increase their own power.

Penny was expected back on Tuesday and I went round to her flat. I waited, but she did not return. Early the next morning I rang Professor Lumsden, who said he had not heard from her for several days. When I asked for her telephone number in Scotland, he said he was not allowed to give it to me. I was rather puzzled. There seemed to be another mystery here and I began to get worried about Penny.

When I got home I found that the suitcase which I had left behind in Sweden had finally been sent back to me by the Swedish police. That gave me an idea and I drove out to the Ashtons' house at Marlow. The cases which Ashton and Benson had taken to Sweden had also been sent back. I looked at everything very carefully, took everything out of the cases and examined it thoroughly, but found nothing. As I was putting Benson's clothes back into the case, his wallet fell on the floor. I had already examined it once, but this time, when I picked it up, I noticed that the silk lining was torn. I examined it more closely; the lining had been very carefully cut and hidden inside was a piece of paper. I pulled it out. It was a letter:

> To Whom It May Concern
> This letter is carried by Howard Greatorex Benson.
> If anyone has any doubts or questions about his
> honesty, his actions or his motives, please contact
> me immediately.

The date on the letter was 4th January 1947, the day
Ashton and Benson had left the army. The letter was signed
by James Pallton – who was now Lord Cregar.

I was getting more and more suspicious about Cregar.
Why did his name keep coming up in the Ashton case? I
could now see that there was a strong connection between
him and Ashton's probable work on genetics – and now
Lumsden and Penny. What exactly was going on in Scotland?
I went to see Lumsden and asked him to ring Penny in
Scotland. When he refused, I got angry. He would not tell
me where the laboratory was, or what work was being done
there, or even who ran it. I was now very suspicious and
finally got Lumsden to admit that Cregar was the man in
charge. Cregar was in a hurry to get results. Penny had
insisted on a P4 laboratory which was much more expensive
and would take much more time to construct.

'But that was because she was worried about safety,' I
said.

'Yes, but Cregar thought she was being too careful. He
was pushing Carter hard to get results fast,' replied
Lumsden.

'Who's Carter?' I wanted to know.

'The Chief Scientific Officer.'

'There's something wrong at that laboratory, I'm sure of

it,' I said. 'Please telephone Penny – but I don't think they'll let you speak to her.'

He hesitated for a long time, but then made the call. As he dialled, I watched his finger and carefully remembered the number.

'This is Professor Lumsden. I'd like to speak to Dr Ashton. Yes, I'll wait while you get her.' He put his hand over the telephone and said, 'They've gone to get her. They think she's in her room.'

'I don't think they'll find her,' I said.

Suddenly Lumsden spoke again to the telephone. 'Yes? . . . on the mainland. I see. Will you ask her to telephone me as soon as she comes back?'

He put the phone down slowly. 'They say she's gone to the mainland.'

'So the laboratory's on an island?'

'Yes,' he said. 'They could be right, you know. They might be telling the truth.' But I could tell from his voice that he did not really believe his own words.

'I don't think so,' I replied. 'Something has happened to her, and I'm going to find out what it is.'

Feeling very worried, I left Lumsden and went to see Ogilvie. I marched straight into his office. He was not pleased.

'I didn't send for you,' he said coldly.

I paid no attention. 'I've discovered Benson's secret,' I said. 'He was Cregar's man.'

Ogilvie's eyes opened wide. 'I don't believe it.'

I put the letter on his desk. 'Read that. You'll see how Benson was Cregar's spy on Ashton for thirty years. Even when Cregar was no longer responsible for Ashton, he still had his spy watching. That's why Benson's records disappeared from the computer.'

'It all fits together,' admitted Ogilvie, 'but I still can't believe it. There must be another explanation.'

'Well, I'll get it out of Cregar, even if I have to beat it out of him. Penny Ashton has disappeared and Cregar has something to do with it.'

'What on earth are you talking about?' he demanded.

I told him about Penny's work in Scotland and how Cregar was involved in this secret laboratory. I gave him the phone number and said, 'See if you can find out where that telephone is.'

Five minutes later he had the answer in two words, 'Cladach Duillich'.

14

Trouble in Scotland

Cladach Duillich was a hard place to get to. It was one of the Summer Islands, off the north-west coast of Scotland, islands which are beautiful in summer and terrible in winter. I flew to Inverness and hired a car to drive across Scotland to Ullapool, the nearest fishing village to Cladach Duillich.

It was late when I arrived but I found a small hotel quite easily. I managed to find a fisherman who promised to take me to Cladach Duillich the next morning, if the weather was right.

Before dinner I sat in the bar talking with the local people. They did not know much about what happened on Cladach Duillich. There were a few buildings, that was all, but the people who worked there always came and went by helicopter. They never came to Ullapool. Nobody else was allowed to land on the island.

'What do you think they're doing there?' I asked. 'Do you think it's another Gruinard?'

Gruinard was a Scottish island where a government experiment in biological weapons had gone very wrong many years ago. The island had been badly poisoned and was still too dangerous for anyone to go there.

'It had better not be,' said a man called Archie Ferguson angrily. He was a tall, powerful Scot, with a soft voice and a fierce-looking face. 'If we thought it was another Gruinard,' he went on, 'we'd take the fire to it and burn everything to the ground.'

After dinner I made a telephone call to Cladach Duillich. A voice said, 'How can I help you?'

'I'd like to speak to Dr Ashton. My name is Malcolm Jaggard.'

'Just a moment. I'll see if she's available,' came the reply.

There was a four-minute silence, then another voice said, 'I'm sorry, Mr Jaggard, but Dr Ashton went to the mainland and hasn't come back yet.'

'Whereabouts on the mainland?' I asked.

There was a pause. 'Where are you speaking from, Mr Jaggard?'

'From London. Why?'

The voice did not answer the question. 'She went to

Ullapool – that's our nearest town. She wanted to do some shopping. May I ask how you got our number?'

'Dr Ashton gave it to me,' I lied. 'When do you expect her back?'

'Oh, I don't know. The weather has changed and I don't think she'll be able to get a boat back to the island until tomorrow morning. I'm sure she'll be back then.'

'I see. May I ask who I'm speaking to?'

'I'm Dr Carter.'

'Thank you, Dr Carter. I'll ring tomorrow.'

As I put the phone down, I knew that I was not the only person who was telling lies. I went back to the bar and spoke to Archie Ferguson again.

'I've been talking to the people on Cladach Duillich. They told me a woman came to Ullapool today from the island. She's about one metre seventy tall, dark hair, about twenty-eight years old.'

Robbie Ferguson, Archie's brother, interrupted me. 'How did she come from the island?'

'By boat,' I answered.

'Then she didn't come,' he said positively. 'There's no boat on Cladach Duillich – only a helicopter. Nobody came from the island to Ullapool today, I can promise you that.'

The next morning Robbie Ferguson's boat took me across the rough seas to Cladach Duillich. It was a low island which looked as if the sea could cover it at any time. Before I left, I said to Archie, 'Look, if I'm not back by four o'clock this afternoon, I want you to get the police and come looking for me.'

'And if they won't let us land on the island? What do we do then?' he wanted to know.

I took a card from my pocket and gave it to him. 'If I don't come back, ring that number and ask for a man called Ogilvie. Tell him everything you know.'

'I'll do that. And maybe we'll come with fire to make Cladach Duillich clean again. Fire is a great thing for destroying what is bad.'

I did not argue with him but, as Robbie and I approached Cladach Duillich, I felt better knowing that I had Archie Ferguson behind me in case anything went wrong. He was a dependable man.

It was a rough voyage across the sea to Cladach Duillich. Although it was not a high island, the sharp rocks made it a difficult place to land. I could not think of any reason why anyone should want to build a biological laboratory there, unless they had something which they very much wanted to hide.

Robbie Ferguson brought the boat in as close as he could, and I jumped on to the rocky shore. I saw a notice:

GOVERNMENT PROPERTY
Landing forbidden

It did not say who had forbidden everyone to land on the island.

There were some steps leading from the rocks where I had landed. When I got to the top, a man came running up.

'Stop! Can't you read?' he shouted.

'Yes, I can read. But the boat's gone.'

'Well, you can't stay here. What do you want?'

It was a rough voyage across the sea to Cladach Duillich.

'I want to talk to Dr Carter,' I replied.

'What about?'

'If Dr Carter wants you to know what we talk about, I'm sure he'll tell you later,' I said sharply.

'Who are you?' the man said angrily.

'Same answer,' I replied. 'Just take me to Carter.'

Very unhappily he took me along the path to the buildings of the laboratory, and I took a look around.

Cladach Duillich was a small island where only the sea-birds seemed to be at home. There were three low buildings, all connected. I was taken into an office where an older man was sitting, working at a desk. He looked up as we entered.

'Who's this, Max?'

'I found this man coming ashore. He says he wants to see you.'

He turned to me. 'Who are you? What do you want?'

I sat down. 'I'm Malcolm Jaggard. I've come to see Dr Ashton.'

'Didn't you ring me last night? I told you she wasn't here – she's on the mainland, in Ullapool.'

'No, she isn't. I've just come from there. And she wasn't there last night either,' I said firmly.

'Well, she isn't here now,' he said. 'And I must ask you to leave. This place isn't open to the public.'

'If Dr Ashton isn't here, where is she? How did she get to Ullapool?'

'By boat, of course.'

'But you haven't got a boat here, Dr Carter. All journeys are by helicopter.'

'You're taking too much of an interest in us, Mr Jaggard. That could be dangerous.'

'Just let Dr Ashton come and talk to me,' I replied. 'If she's missing, I promise that I'll make a lot of trouble for you.'

A voice came from behind me. 'Dr Carter can't bring Dr Ashton to see you.'

I turned and saw Lord Cregar in the doorway.

'Dr Carter, leave me to talk to Mr Jaggard alone,' he went on. He turned to the man I had met outside and who had brought me in. 'Search him, Max. Make sure he hasn't got a gun.'

'No gun,' said Max, after he had searched me carefully.

'Oh well, even if he hasn't got a gun, he could still get drowned if he was on the island, trying to break into these buildings, couldn't he?' said Cregar calmly.

'No problem, sir,' said Max unfeelingly. 'The waves sometimes break right over the island.'

'You'd better be careful, Lord Cregar,' I said. 'We've found the connection between you and Benson.'

Cregar looked surprised. 'How could I have a connection with Benson? What possible evidence could there be?'

'A letter carried by Benson, dated January, 1947, and signed by you.'

'A letter?' said Cregar, and he looked through me into the past. His eyes changed as he began to remember. 'You mean Benson still carried that letter with him, after thirty years. I don't believe it. Where is it now?'

'Ogilvie has it. He's probably shown it to the Minister by now.'

Cregar was angry. 'I'm not going to let you beat me, Jaggard. Max, put this man somewhere safe while I think. I've found my way out of bigger problems than this. It's a question of studying the weaknesses of each man – you and Ogilvie.'

'What about Penny Ashton?' I said angrily. 'What's happened to her?'

'You'll see her in good time,' said Cregar coldly, 'if I allow you to.'

In my anger I wanted to attack him violently, but Max had a gun in his hand so I could do nothing. I was taken along a corridor and into a small, dark room. The door closed heavily behind me, and I was left alone, in the dark, to think about my problems.

I realized that it had been a good idea to tell Cregar about the letter. That had saved me. Before I had mentioned the letter, Cregar was thinking of having me thrown into the sea, but the knowledge that Ogilvie had the letter had stopped that plan. But I now had a very clear idea of just how dangerous Cregar could be.

I was in that black room for many hours, but finally the door opened. Max was there, with his gun, and safely behind him stood Cregar, looking relaxed.

'Come with me,' he said, and I followed him along the corridor with Max walking behind me, his gun in his hand.

'I've found a way of dealing with Ogilvie – there'll be no problem there,' said Cregar casually. 'But that still leaves you. After you've seen Dr Ashton, we'll have a talk.' He stopped at a door. 'In here,' he said.

I went into a room with a large window, which looked into another room. There was a bed in that room and a woman was lying in the bed, unconscious, with plastic tubes leading from her to various machines. I could hardly recognize my Penny.

'In God's name, what happened?' I shouted at Cregar.

'There was an accident last week. I'm afraid Dr Ashton is rather ill.'

'What's wrong with her?' I shouted again.

'We don't know. It's something new, and Carter can't identify it.'

I was very angry and very frightened for Penny. 'It's your fault, isn't it? She wanted you to have a P4 laboratory, and you were too mean. This place isn't safe. Why isn't she being properly looked after? She should be in a hospital, one of the best hospitals.'

'You're probably right,' said Cregar calmly. 'But that would create risks for me – not health risks, but risks of security. This is a top-secret laboratory.'

'But you can't leave her to die here. She needs to have the very best of medical treatment,' I shouted at Cregar.

'You're in no position to make demands of me,' said Cregar, and walked out. I followed him along the corridor to Carter's laboratory. We went inside, through an airlock between two doors. There were glass cases all round the walls, containing small dishes with Carter's experimental bacteria. Each dish was in its own protective glass box.

Cregar turned to me, 'Look, you can see we do take care here. What happened to Dr Ashton was an accident, a million to one chance. It's very important to me that you believe me.'

'If you'd listened to her, it wouldn't have happened,' I said, 'but I believe you. I don't think it was done on purpose. What's so important about what I think, anyway?'

'Well, I can come to an agreement with Ogilvie. But I still have to make sure you don't give away my secrets.'

'Have you spoken with Ogilvie?' I asked.

'Yes, of course. He understands.'

I felt sick with disgust. Even Ogilvie seemed to be willing to hide the truth, to allow himself to be bribed by this dangerous government official. I knew then that I would never work with Ogilvie again.

'The trouble is that you have to be around, Jaggard, for

some time to come. If anything happened to you, Ogilvie might change his mind. That's too great a risk, and it creates a problem for me.'

'How to keep my mouth shut without actually killing me?'

'Exactly. You are a man like myself – we go straight to the heart of any problem. But I think we can do business. I'll exchange the life of Dr Ashton for your silence.'

I looked at Cregar with total disgust. He had said that the solution to his problem would be found by studying men's weaknesses, and he had found mine.

'As soon as you agree, Dr Ashton can be taken to hospital. There's a document I want you to sign – it'll make sure that you remain silent.'

A telephone rang. Cregar told Max to give him the gun and then answer the call. There was silence as Max listened, saying only, 'Who? Where? How many?'

He put the phone down. 'There's trouble outside. A lot of men are landing on the island.'

'Who are they?' said Cregar.

'Local people.'

'Stupid Scots fishermen. Go and chase them away, Max.'

As Max left, Cregar turned to me and asked, 'Is this any-thing to do with you?'

'How could I start a local war?' I asked. 'But I want Penny in hospital fast. How do we get off here?'

'A phone call will bring a helicopter in two hours.'

'You'd better make that phone call then,' I replied.

While he was thinking about what I had just said, I hit him hard in the stomach. As he fell to the floor, his gun went off;

the bullet missed me, but I heard the crash of breaking glass.

By the time he picked himself up, I was holding the gun.

'What's the number to ring for the helicopter?' I said.

'You can't win, Jaggard,' shouted Cregar. 'Nobody will ever believe your word rather than mine.'

He turned his head, noticed the broken glass and screamed, 'Oh God! Look what you've done. I'm getting out of here!'

Two of the glass cases in the laboratory were broken and the contents of the dishes had spilled on the floor. Cregar tried to push past me to get out of the room. He did not seem to care about the gun, so I hit him over the head and he fell to the floor, unconscious.

I turned quickly as the door of the laboratory burst open and Archie Ferguson appeared.

'Get out!' I shouted. 'Get out! It's not safe. Go next door and I'll talk to you.'

The door shut very quickly and a moment later I saw Archie through the glass window of Carter's laboratory. Cregar still lay unconscious at my feet.

15

Biological disaster

There was a microphone on one of the tables in Carter's laboratory. I picked it up with a shaking hand and spoke, 'Can you hear me, Archie?'

He nodded and picked up another microphone.

'What's happened here, Malcolm?' he asked.

'This place is bloody dangerous, Archie. Don't go into any of the laboratories – go and tell your men that, *now*!'

Archie dropped the microphone and ran off quickly to tell his men. After a few minutes he came back and I told him to arrest everybody on the island. I showed him my official identity card and said, 'That gives you the power to arrest people. The Government will support that. You're working under my instructions.'

'What do we do now?' he wanted to know.

'Ring Ogilvie and let me speak to him. I daren't come out of this laboratory. I don't know what experiments they're doing here, but the bacteria we've accidentally released are almost certainly very dangerous.'

When I turned round, Cregar was starting to wake up, but he said nothing. The call to Ogilvie came through. Before he could start asking questions, I said sharply, 'This is an emergency. Cregar's laboratory has gone wrong. There's one serious case of infection, and two suspected cases. The bacteria causing it are new to medicine, probably man-made, and highly infectious. We need immediate hospital treatment for three people in P4 conditions. I suggest the biological centre at Porton Down.'

'I'll get that arranged at once,' said Ogilvie. 'Who are the three people in danger?'

'The serious case is Penelope Ashton.'

There was a gasp at the other end of the line. 'Oh, my God! I'm sorry, Malcolm,' came Ogilvie's voice.

I went on. 'The suspected cases are Cregar and myself.'

'*This is an emergency. Cregar's laboratory has gone wrong.*'

'For God's sake, Malcolm! What's been happening up there?'

'You'd better ask Dr Carter. He's the man in charge of the experiments up here. But make it quick. I think Penny is dying.'

When I had finished talking to Ogilvie, Archie Ferguson picked up his microphone. He had been listening to the conversation and was very angry. He wanted to throw Cregar and the others into the sea, but I persuaded him that that was too dangerous – for the fish. I asked him to find me a cassette-recorder and food for Cregar and me. He was unhappy at the thought of getting food for Cregar, but did it and pushed it into the laboratory.

I got the cassette-recorder ready. Cregar did not seem interested. It was as if he had given up. 'Nothing matters any more,' he said.

'How did Benson learn about Ashton's work?' I asked.

'Oh, that was a long time ago . . . five years ago, at least. He saw that Ashton was helping his daughter with her studies, but also starting to do a lot of work on his own. We never knew what it was. He hid it from Benson and we thought it was hidden in his secret room.' He stopped and looked up at me. 'You're a clever man. I never thought of the railway. I should have done. Ashton wasn't the sort of man to play with toy trains.'

Now that he had started to tell the truth, Cregar's voice flowed on. I suppose he thought there was no reason to keep silent. It was a sort of deathbed confession. I asked him about Mayberry's attack on Gillian.

'I had nothing to do with that,' said Cregar. 'It was senseless. I didn't even know Mayberry existed until the police found him. But I was ready to take advantage of it. I had the flat in Stockholm ready, and the false passport. It only needed Benson to persuade Ashton that his girls were in danger and that my department had a safe house for him in Sweden. He ran away. All I wanted to do was look in his secret room, but it was empty.'

I began to see why so many misunderstandings had happened. Ashton had never known the truth, and neither had I. 'But why on earth did Benson kill Ashton?'

'Orders from thirty years ago, to make sure Ashton didn't go back to the Russians. I never thought to cancel the order and Benson remembered it after all those years. I can hardly believe it!' Cregar seemed almost proud of Benson's loyalty – even though it had led to Ashton's unnecessary death.

Out of curiosity, I asked, 'Cregar, why did you do all this?'

He looked at me in surprise. 'A man must do something important in his life – something that people will remember.'

I stared at him and felt cold to my bones. He carried on talking about power and politics, but I was no longer interested. Finally Ogilvie rang to say there was a helicopter with a specialist medical team on its way to us.

The men who came were dressed in plastic clothing, from head to foot, just like men from space. They put us in plastic envelopes and carried us away to hospital. I never saw Cregar again.

16

My new job

A month later I came out of the special hospital where a team of thirty doctors and nurses had looked after me. Penny had even more doctors than I had because her condition was worse than mine, but Ogilvie and Lumsden had brought the best doctors from the United States and from Europe, and they had succeeded in saving Penny's life.

Dr Starkie was the man in charge. 'If Dr Ashton had been on Cladach Duillich for one more day without proper medical attention, she would be dead now,' he said. 'You were both very lucky.'

Slowly Penny began to get better. I couldn't kiss her, or even touch her in her protective glass cage, but we began to talk about getting married. She said she thought a double wedding would be nice – Michaelis had asked Gillian to marry him. I was not too surprised at that piece of news.

Ogilvie had come to visit me in hospital.

'I've listened to the cassette of your conversation with Cregar,' he said. 'I don't think even Cregar can escape from this problem.'

'Have the computer experts had any success with Ashton's computer programs?' I asked.

'Yes, and my God, they're fantastic! Everyone said the man was a genius and he's proved it.'

'How is that? What's he done?'

'Well, I don't really understand it,' said Ogilvie, 'but it

seems that Ashton has done for genetics what Einstein did for physics. He studied genetics from a mathematical point of view, and has shown that genetics has a mathematical basis. He's been able to show what genetic arrangements are possible or not possible, without depending on laboratory experiments for each arrangement. It's quite fantastic.'

'That should make Professor Lumsden happy,' I said.

'He doesn't know,' said Ogilvie. 'The information is still secret.'

'Why?'

'The Minister thinks that there are good reasons for keeping it secret, at least for a while. We have to study how useful the information could be.'

I felt disgusted. The Minister was another Cregar. He had found a piece of important information and that gave him power as long as it was secret. He was going to hold on to it. I began to realize why Ashton had hidden his ideas; it was to keep them away from men like Cregar and the Minister.

Ogilvie went on. 'When you've fully recovered and get back to work, I've got a new job for you. I want to prepare you for Kerr's job. He's going to retire in two years, and you're the right man for the job.'

Kerr was number two to Ogilvie in the Department.

'When I retire in seven years' time,' Ogilvie continued, 'you could be head of the Department.'

'Get lost!' I said bluntly. 'I don't want the job.'

Ogilvie was shocked. 'What did you say? What's got into you, Malcolm?'

'You weren't interested in what was right or wrong. You were going to do a deal with Cregar. He told me he had come to an agreement with you. I was shocked. Cregar called me an honest man – but to Cregar that isn't a good thing. It just meant he didn't know how to buy me. He could buy everyone else so that they would do what he said – even you! That's why I don't want your job. I might become like you. How could an honest man do what we did to George Ashton?'

'Malcolm, I don't think that you're being sensible about this,' he replied angrily.

'I'm a human being. I try to be honest, and I want to stay that way. Your job would destroy that part of me.'

Ogilvie went away very unhappy.

17

The future

And we all lived happily ever after. At least, that's what would have happened in the old-fashioned kind of story we all used to read when we were children.

But my story is different.

Penny came out of hospital fully recovered. Gillian came back from New York looking better than she had before the acid attack. Together with Michaelis we all went out for dinner and planned a wonderful double wedding.

Ten days before the wedding I went back to see Dr Starkie. He asked me a lot of questions, gave me a lot of medical tests, and told me to come back in a week.

On the day I went back to see him, I read in *The Times* that

Lord Cregar had died. I was disgusted by what was written about him. 'A loyal public servant who worked for his country for many years with no thought for himself.' That was not the Cregar who had been quite prepared to let Penny and me die on Cladach Duillich in order to save himself.

Dr Starkie was very serious when I saw him.

'It's bad news, isn't it?' I said.

'Yes, it is,' he said directly. 'It's cancer.'

It was the news I had expected. 'How long have I got?'

'Six months. Maybe a year. It could be longer, but not much.'

'Is this the same thing that killed Cregar?' I asked.

'Yes,' he sighed. 'Cregar wanted fast results and Carter didn't wait for the best quality materials to come from the States. He used some experimental bacteria which were difficult to control biologically. And he didn't have the right kind of laboratory – Penny Ashton was right there. The new bacteria that escaped when you and Cregar were in the laboratory weren't safe.'

I suddenly felt frightened. 'What about Penny?'

'She's all right. Her illness was caused by completely different bacteria.'

I felt relieved. 'Thank you, Dr Starkie. You've been very honest with me, and I appreciate it.'

I went back to London and told Penny the bad news. She understood immediately what had happened – it was her job, after all. She still wanted to get married, but I said no. I knew what I wanted to do.

'There's a place in the south of Ireland,' I said to Penny. 'The mountains are green, the sea is blue when the sun shines, and it's green when the sun doesn't shine. It's by the

sea, where the Atlantic waves come in from the west. Come
live with me and be my love. I could do with six months of
life there, if you are with me.'

We went to Ireland immediately after Gillian and Peter
were married, and we wished them every happiness.

We have lived here for nine months. My condition has got
gradually worse, and at one time I thought of killing myself,
but I knew I had one final job to do, to write the story of the
Ashton case.

Penny has loved me and taken care of me. She has
brought a doctor and three nurses to help her, but now my
time is getting short.

I have told the story honestly. God knows, I am not proud
of my own part in it. Penny has read the story; some parts
have upset her terribly, some parts have made her laugh,
other parts have made her sad. She has typed it all herself.

I want people to be able to read my story, to know what is
done by governments in the name of 'the people'. There are
too many Cregars around in government. Ashton's new
work on genetics is still a secret, to be used for whatever
purposes some government minister thinks will do him
some good. Because of that Penny and I are determined that
her father's story and the news of his discoveries in genetics
should not be hidden. We have done what we can to make
sure that the story will be published in full.

This story, and my life, are now coming to an end. It is
not a happy story. In the words of an American writer: 'We
have met the enemy, and he is us.'

I hope, for your sake, that he is wrong.

Exercises

A Checking your understanding

Chapters 1–7 *Find answers to these questions in the text.*

1 Why did Penny invite Malcolm to spend the weekend at her home?
2 What happened to Gillian Ashton on Malcolm's second visit?
3 What did George Ashton want Malcolm to do?
4 Why was Malcolm surprised by the first message on the computer screen?
5 What did Ogilvie want Malcolm to do?
6 What surprising things did Malcolm find in the Ashtons' house?
7 Why did Penny and Malcolm quarrel?
8 Why did Aleksandr Chelyuskin decide to leave Russia?
9 Why were the British disappointed with Chelyuskin?

Chapters 8–12 *Are these sentences true (T) or false (F)?*

1 Gillian would always be completely blind.
2 Peter Mayberry admitted that he had hired a car in Slough.
3 The book on genetics gave Malcolm a clue to Mayberry's motives.
4 Mayberry's attack on Gillian had no connection with George Ashton.
5 Ogilvie didn't care if Ashton went back to Russia.
6 Malcolm did not agree with Ogilvie's plan, but he had to do what Ogilvie told him.
7 The man who killed Ashton was not the real Howard Benson.

Chapters 13–17 *Write answers to these questions.*

1 How did Ashton keep his studies and his work in genetics hidden from outsiders?
2 Why was Malcolm worried about Cregar's interest in Ashton's computer programs?
3 What did the hidden letter in Benson's wallet prove?
4 Why did Malcolm go to Scotland?
5 What was the bargain that Cregar wanted to make with Malcolm?
6 Why didn't Malcolm dare to go out of the laboratory after Cregar's gun had gone off?
7 Why didn't Malcolm want Ogilvie's job?
8 Why did Malcolm want his story to be published?

B Working with language

1 *Choose the best linking word and complete these sentences with information from the story.*

1 The Ashton family had a peaceful existence until/after . . .
2 Malcolm was told to guard Ashton unless/although . . .
3 Even though/Because Ashton thought his daughters were in danger, . . .
4 Malcolm could not search Ashton's house unless/so Penny . . .
5 Malcolm told Ogilvie he would resign when/if . . .

2 *Put this summary in the right order and then join the parts together to make five sentences.*

1 Malcolm pretended to agree and then attacked him
2 who told him that Penny was in Ullapool
3 and soon he, Penny, and Cregar were flown to hospital by helicopter
4 so the next morning he went by boat to Cladach Duillich
5 However, Cregar's gun went off by accident
6 Malcolm knew that wasn't true
7 When Malcolm arrived in Ullapool in Scotland
8 and when Lord Cregar tried to buy his silence
9 He found that Penny was dangerously ill
10 which released some dangerous experimental bacteria
11 he telephoned Dr Carter
12 Malcolm then telephoned Ogilvie in London to demand help
13 and smashed some glass cases

C Activities

1 Write a short description of a character that you like in the story.
2 After Malcolm buys Ashton's model railway for £31,000, he has to explain to his boss Ogilvie why he did it. At first Ogilvie thinks Malcolm is crazy. Imagine their conversation and write it down.
3 The novel gives a depressing picture of the relationship between science and politics. Do you think it is a true picture? Why, or why not? Do you think that scientists should be controlled by politicians? Write a short essay, giving your opinions.

Glossary

acid a liquid chemical that can burn what it touches

airlock a small room with an airtight door at each end

auction a sale where each thing is sold to the person who offers the most money for it

bacteria the simplest and smallest forms of life, which are often a cause of disease

biology the scientific study of all living things, plants, and animals

bloody a swear-word used to express anger

cancer a diseased growth in the body, which often causes death

career a person's working life and its progress or development

CIA Central Intelligence Agency (the spy and secret intelligence organization of the USA)

coincidence when two similar things happen at the same time by chance

damn a word to express impatience or anger

devil a very wicked person; also used for emphasis in questions, e.g. *What the devil are you doing?*

economist a person who studies the management of a country's finance and business

fingerprint mark made by a finger on a surface and used for identifying people

fit in good health because of regular physical exercise

gene an extremely small chemical unit which passes qualities from parents to children

genetics the study of genes and how they work

genius a person of exceptional intelligence or creative ability

idiot a foolish person

lining the soft, thin material on the inside of clothing, a wallet, etc.

lord a title for a man of noble family

mathematics the science of numbers

mechanical working by machine

monster an animal or plant that is unnatural or abnormal in some way

outsider a person who is not a member of a particular group, society, family, etc.

physics the scientific study of light, heat, sound, electricity, etc.

professor a university teacher of the highest level

publish to print copies of something written and offer them for sale

Glossary

research detailed study to discover new facts or knowledge

security the protection of secret information against spying and theft

strong-room a room with thick walls and doors, where valuables are kept

tap (*v*) to fix a piece of equipment to a telephone line in order to listen secretly to people's conversations

tragedy a terrible event that causes great sadness

tube a long, hollow, soft pipe for carrying liquids

virus a simple organism, smaller than bacteria, which causes infectious diseases